The Inland Ground

Richard Rhodes

The Inland Ground

An Evocation of
the American Middle West

Illustrations by Bill Greer

New York

Atheneum

1970

Five of the chapters in this book have been published previously in magazine form. "Death All Day" appeared in Esquire under the title "Death All Day in Kansas," and "Harry's Last Hurrah," "Behold, How Good and How Pleasant It Is for Brethren to Dwell Together in Unity," An Artist in Iron," and "Watching the Animals" were published in Harper's Magazine.

Excerpts from At Ease by Dwight D. Eisenhower, copyright © 1967 by Dwight D. Eisenhower, are reprinted by permission of Doubleday & Company, Inc. Lines from "A Primitive Like an Orb," from The Collected Poems of Wallace Stevens, copyright © 1954 by Wallace Stevens, are reprinted by permission of Alfred A. Knopf, Inc. Selections from the writings of Jesse Howard are quoted by permission of Mr. Howard.

For *Linda,* *with thanks to* G.A.E.

Contents

Contents

The Inland Ground

1 *The Inland Ground:*
An Introduction

THE MIDDLE WEST WAS LAND BEFORE IT WAS PEOPLE, A BROAD inland ground. To the south, alluvial; to the north, glacial; to the east, forested; to the west, dry and barren of trees. A vastness, a wilderness. Once an ocean floor, now the basin of a great river. Rimmed by mountain ranges. Only slowly settled, and not settled yet. A place of many places, too many for one book: what follows must be only a sampling, Kansas, Missouri, something of Nebraska and Iowa. The black dirt and prairie west, the Middle West I know.

Many, when they first saw the prairies, looking out from the forest of the Middle Border, called them a sea. That is how they would look to seaboard eyes, but they were a sea you could walk on. Their essence was their boundlessness: they extended to the horizon, hardly interrupted by trees or hills. Onto such blankness each visitor could project his own interior landscape, and did, some calling the prairies the Great American Desert, others the Garden of the World. Both were right—are right today about the entire Middle West, culturally as well as geographically. Culturally a desert, if by culture one means the high European forms; culturally a garden if by culture one means the broad vernacular forms, if one means sources, if one means the talented young. A coyote hunt has its esthetic, as formal as any bullfight. Missouri on the Mississippi produced both Mark Twain and T. S. Eliot, not a bad list for any state's canon. Iowa grows poets as sturdy as its corn. Independence, Missouri, raised Harry Truman, and Abilene, Kansas, raised Dwight Eisenhower. In St. Louis, two Midwesterners explore the farther shores of sexuality. And the Middle West has delivered its young to the great turnstile cities of the East and Far West long enough to qualify, like Great Britain, as a region suffering from the emigration of its best minds.

Like Florida, with its interior swamps and its circumferential ring of cities, the United States itself is polarizing on its east and west coasts. The Middle West is not yet losing population, but neither is it gaining at anything like the rate of increase of the two coasts. It is a region most coastal people fly over, and even the natives who live here, more and more of them, speak of moving away. The Middle West's cities have aged; its farm population has declined; and only its anonymous suburbs, as in the rest of the United States, have temporarily prospered. At what terrible expense to the human spirit who can say?

And perhaps the Middle West is not a place at all, is too dispersed over the vastness of its lands to generate any sense of permanence in its children. We were never a steady people, but moved on to the next range of open land if we didn't like the land we settled, or had used it up. Our western range

4

was among the last land to be settled in the United States. Pioneers preferred the difficult and dangerous pilgrimage to Oregon and California. Iowa was settled soon enough, but Iowa has never seemed to me to be typical of this region: more a demonstration farm than a place; more some cosmic public-relations project designed to prove that God's in his heaven and all's right with the world. Missouri joins all that is worst—and best—of North and South into one Gothic rural ruin (except for St. Louis, a French city prefabricated in New Orleans and shipped up the Mississippi two hundred years ago by fur traders); Kansas sits as strait-laced as some country church; Nebraska stretches out flat and parsimonious and plain; but Iowa might have been buttered, it is so sleek. And how many different places have I already mentioned, and hardly begun to mention all the places of the Middle West?

My Middle West, which this book is more or less about, with some important omissions and some wanderings off over the hill, was Kansas City, Missouri, and Independence, Missouri. It is a country lake in Kansas as I write. During the years of World War II, we—my widower father, my brother, and I—moved all over the east side of Kansas City, a lower-middle-class area which is now part of the city's black ghetto, living in boardinghouses and occasionally a real home. I was cared for by German immigrants who believed in education, hard widows who knew how to bread a meat loaf, middle-class mothers in need of extra income, and spinsters heavy with love. If anyone raised me, my older brother did. We lived in the streets, flattening bottle caps on streetcar tracks, walking the high parapets of outdoor billboards, occupying vacant lots, wandering the huge storm sewers that drain Kansas City's rainwater into the Missouri River. We saw *Lassie Come Home* at the National Theater on Independence Avenue and cried, and later saw *Frankenstein* there at night and hardly dared the shadowed walk home. Old Mr. Gernhardt, a

5

German POW from World War I who stayed to become an American citizen, told us of helping to build the Al-Can Highway and sang "Mademoiselle from Armentières" at the piano until Mrs. Gernhardt stopped him.

Unable to find a school library book in my fourth-grade year, I stole a five-dollar bill from my father, bought a box of kitchen matches and a package of notebook paper at the corner drugstore, and rode by bus and trolley on a school morning in the wintertime to Swope Park, determined to become a wise and much-consulted hermit there. Climbed the wooded hill to a clearing behind the bronze statue of Colonel Swope, wadded up the notepaper, and lit it. Found no warmth but some wisdom, retraced my path back to school and accepted the principal's mild scolding and my father's amusement. He paid for the book.

We tended no Victory Garden, being renters only, but collected grease and flattened tin cans to help the war effort. The Manor bread man drove through the neighborhood three times a week in a truck pulled by a horse and gave us—a gang of children long ago dispersed and their names forgotten—day-old sweet rolls. And though my brother and I were lonely, those days seem now some paradise for the city and for me. The war occupied adult attentions and eliminated distracting luxuries: with little gasoline available to automobiles, the streets were ours, and a glorious afternoon in midsummer might be magic as simple as a hike up the hill to the Velvet Freeze ice-cream parlor for a butterscotch sundae.

Later, my father remarried, and all our lives for a time became painful. Still the city spared us. Told to leave the house in the morning and not return until night, we biked to the eight-foot trailer of an old woman who lived in a vacant lot beside a creek. She had a cigarette-making machine, and would roll cigarettes for us along with her own. Once she baked a moist, raisiny cake on her hot plate which the three of us ate at one sitting. In her prime she roamed the back-roads in her trailer taking portrait photographs of country people. Now she was old, and lived on the little money her son could send her.

And other distractions: school friends; long bike tours to green city parks; watching the doughnut-making machine at the Katz drugstore; reading at the library; selling Christmas cards door to door to earn a chemistry set; swimming at the city pool.

And abruptly, when I was twelve and my brother fourteen, in the summer of 1949, we were removed to the country, to a boys' home run under a private trust, the Andrew Drumm Institute in Independence, Missouri, and found ourselves farmers. Neither of us took easily to farming, having lived in the city as urban Huckleberry Finns, but we had no choice, and so we learned that work, never with the inborn sense of routine that a child raised on a farm possesses, but with some fair imitation of it.

Began cleaning chicken roosts for chores, leading the old mare in and out of the barn to raise and lower the hay hook, straightening whole kegs of nails salvaged from a razed shed, hoeing the forty-acre garden, picking strawberries, planting potatoes, filling up, when the train bell atop the smokehouse called us to supper, on heavy country food. Learning, later, to plow and disk and mow; to feed cattle and clean the barn; to cook for forty people and clean the dormitories; to cut down trees; to weld; to speak in public and conduct a parliamentary meeting; to operate a mangle and a steam press; to drive a school bus and a farm truck; to show a steer and a sheep; to butcher cattle and hogs and chickens; to can tomatoes and cut meat; to paint fences and build a barn; to call hogs and terrace a field; to deliver calves; to dock lambs; to put up silage in the sweet sweaty silo and grind corn in the violent

7

hammer mill. Learning besides to play football and baseball and basketball; to run track; learning plane geometry and algebra and world history; learning vocational agriculture: the anatomy of farm animals, their diseases, their breeding, seeds, crops, fertilizers, woodwork, metalwork, electricity, plumbing, engines, farm machinery.

Feeling at times, in the isolation of adolescence, despair of my past and despair of my future, but never able to sustain such despair for long because the land and the animals and the work always called me back to those things that must be done next, to those daily regularities that insist on the continuation and preservation of the world. Cows must be milked, and animals fed, and these are certainties on which even loneliness must found an alleviation.

We also discovered other things to do. Tried wine-making, one summer, without benefit of text. Our young scientist built a still, but most of us crushed grapes and mixed in what were probably fatal doses of yeast and stolen sugar. Charlie Frakes, our slow bully whom I made my friend, I came across one night in the workshop boiling dry field corn in a number-ten can. We boiled it together, for two hours, but it was hardly soft even then. Charlie took the stew and loaded it with sugar and hid the mess in the hayloft. Word finally reached our agriculture instructor, who lived at the home with his wife, and he declared amnesty on a full-mooned summer night and found his small back porch covered the next morning with Mason jars and tin cans filled with God knows what strange growths. We smoked grapevines, pungent as Gauloises, or crushed autumn leaves rolled in corn-silk. I spent whole Saturday afternoons with a truncheon of a magazine waging war on the wasps that occupied our dormitory's front porch, killing more than a hundred in one energetic day. Some of the boys, tired of the marauding cats which crowded around the milkhouse door at separating time, would corner the screeching beasts inside the building and hose them down. Charlie liked to toss the sixteen-pound shotput and watch a mongrel dog—we kept a pack of them around for love and garbage—attempt to retrieve it across the playing field. Or we would sled down the hill in the south pasture, jumping the creek bed at the risk of breaking our young necks. Or steal vitamin-C tablets, sweet as lemonade, from the canning house where they were stored in a plastic bag to be used in preserving fresh peaches. Or pocket apples, four winy Jonathans at a time, from the fruit cellar, while loading up a basket of potatoes for the kitchen.

Each year, as a reward for our summer's work of farming, we would pack up and take a long camping trip. Then we saw the land, out beyond the cities. Our bus had a governor and couldn't go more than forty miles an hour, but in it, and trailed by our carry-all, the superintendent's car, and our two-ton truck with a storehouse built onto its bed, we wandered the Middle West and the West for the last month of summer. We took our finest trip during my first summer at the home: across Nebraska to Colorado and Wyoming, to the Grand Canyon, to the Petrified Forest, to Carlsbad, to Santa Fe, through the Texas Panhandle and Oklahoma back to Independence. We followed the Oregon Trail and then dipped south to pick up the Santa Fe Trail, modern Forty-Niners, and every mile of our journey was glorious with freedom from chores and great quenching sights to see. Another year we drove to Yellowstone, which in those days was not as crowded as it has become today, and but for three straight days of rain it was also an extraordinary sight to us, because none of us had ever traveled so before, cooked our meals morning and night over open campfires, fished in clear lakes and streams, seen nature in her most fanciful forms.

Yet I came to dislike the region where I lived, learned to look longingly at the ads in *The New Yorker* in the school library and wish I were a part of that world. By the time I left the Middle West, at eighteen, with a scholarship to Yale in my pocket, I was ashamed of where I had grown up. Later I returned, and have lived here these ten years now as an adult, and find nothing to be ashamed of any longer, except my own rejection of the region.

A place and a time are all of a piece, coherent, and you may look anywhere and catch some glimpse of the whole. That is why the chapters that follow discuss such different subjects. Yet when you have read them they should come together to demonstrate something of this region, this place or these places, this inland ground.

Lake of the Forest
February 14, 1970

2 *Some Forebears*

Thomas Jefferson

WHAT HE DID FOR US CANNOT BE MEASURED. AS WASHINGTON
was our first hero, so Jefferson was our first *mind*. There is a
moment early in any enterprise when one man may give such
shape to a region that later men may live and die only within
his frame. Jefferson was that man, and lived at that moment.
Because he understood the continent's extent, and coveted it
all, it was his to do with as he would. Others, like Daniel
Boone, might experience it, but they had no seats in the Star
Chambers of power. Let a young and brilliant man, who
knew what he wanted, sit down and write, and he could have
his way. We were not a country yet, but only a commercial
coast fronting a wilderness. If a young man wants to make an
impression, then let him. England is the problem, not the
wilderness at our back door. Even Franklin, that chattering,

self-important journalist, must have missed the point, or he would certainly have written the Declaration himself, and by the time everyone had finished reading all its maxims and qualifications and asides they would have forgotten its purpose and gone about their business and we would be England's still.

And so young Jefferson held his absolute sway. The young should never be awarded such exception. He was allowed to draft the Declaration. The language, lofted on Lockean clouds, so impressed those high-minded American tradesmen already intimidated by the Virginia accents of Jefferson's voice that they all but gave in, made a few emendations and let the thing go—reserving, thank God, the practicalities of constituting a nation to their own commercial regard. The most handsome face in American history, the perfect eighteenth-century man.

Built Monticello, his little mountain, perfecting it only after his wife's death. Built an Apollonian house, a private, intimate, consciously serene extension of his own shapely body. With homely corners of invention, the weathercock inside, the clock's pendulum disappearing below the floor when it needed winding, the conveyor carrying the pot of nightsoil discreetly from beneath his bed as if the heavy indiscreet body might be tamed if only one were clever enough.

Not knowing what to do with itself, the nation called him back. He sent out Lewis and Clark, and later, in the other direction, Monroe. We might have established a viable coastal civilization and left the interior, as in Africa, to be wandered by explorers and feared by children late at night, but Jefferson would have none of it: he had to find everything out, rationalize it, explain it all and frame a plan for it, lest the wilds overcome his careful defenses. Monroe would not have spent that sixteen million dollars had he not thought President Jefferson would back him up; whatever

Jefferson had officially told him, his spiritual commission was clear, an open hand and an open pocketbook. Monroe back with Livingston and the shocking news, Jefferson conveniently forgot his own deep Constitutional qualms and urged ratification of the Louisiana Purchase, knowing that he was taking severe chances with the still-tender sensibilities of a young nation to make such a recommendation, but arrogant enough, destructive enough, prescient enough to recommend it regardless: because *he* knew best, *his* was the cosmic American consciousness, *he* had invented the United States of America after all, damn Washington and all the others who merely made it work. And turned thereby a militant but straightforward English people who could do nicely, thank you, without George's taxes, into a forlorn people who would spend the next several millennia trying to recover from their expansion and figure out who they were, all because young Tom, young Squire Jefferson, thought he knew best.

He organized the American wilderness, before its details were even mapped, on a grid borrowed from Euclidian geometry: so laid it out despite the fact that he was a countryman who understood curving fields and wandering streams and the vagaries of plantings: laid it out to our eternal complication, his grid the woe of his fellow citizens ever afterward, impossible to find those damned cornerposts, impossible to track those inhuman squares. A Dionysian land, a Dionysian continent, plains and tortuous rivers and sharp mountains and wandering shores, and he overlaid upon it a Euclidian grid as if Apollo truly reigned and the Furies were forever banished.

He socketed his bed into the wall between his bedroom and his study: was that ambivalent, that torn. Our first Kennedy really, as handsome and as outwardly rational and as inwardly Greek: this man caused his stool to be removed by pulleys: this man caused a continent to be penetrated, then

13

bluntly annexed, then measured out in squares. He embodied all the American contradictions: extended his fantasies and his fear of those fantasies out onto the land itself: loved it and hated it, and because of that love and hate saw it uncertainly. Without him we would not have the shame. Without him we would not have the glory. He shaped America. He shaped the inland ground.

Josiah Gregg

JOSIAH GREGG, FRAIL, STUDIOUS SON OF A MISSOURI FARMER, left his home for the prairies of Kansas and the Southwest two months before his twenty-fifth birthday, in May of 1831. A semi-invalid, he suffered from what one of his biographers calls "chronic dyspepsia and consumption." It had confined him to his bedroom for most of the preceding year, until his doctors, all other treatment unavailing, suggested a prairie trip for his health. He signed on as a bookkeeper for a Santa Fe trader operating out of Independence, Missouri.

Two weeks into his first expedition, Gregg had recovered enough to exchange his carriage for a horse—a remarkable healing. In the next nine years Gregg traveled from Independence to Santa Fe and back four times, leading the last expedition and blazing a new trail.

In 1844 Gregg published a book of his travels, *Commerce on the Prairies*. It would go through fourteen printings and become a handbook for travelers and settlers in the regions he described. In 1845, pursuing an old interest, Gregg spent two semesters studying medicine at the University of Louisville, but itched to return to the wilds. The University agreeably awarded him an honorary degree and he again traveled to Santa Fe, had some part in the Mexican War of 1846, went east once more, then returned to Mexico to practice medicine. He could not stay put. After a year he gave over his practice for a botanical exploration through Mexico to California, accepted a commission there to find a bay north of San Francisco lost since early Spanish times, and on that expedition, at the age of forty-four, was killed in a fall from his horse.

Intensely shy, Gregg never married. His hypochondria, though its physical effects subsided, persisted throughout his life. He nagged his men, was impatient of details, was difficult to get along with, especially in his last year; one of his monumental arguments, on that final, fatal expedition, gave California's Mad River its name.

He achieved some scientific distinction: practiced tolerable medicine, drew an excellent map of the prairie regions, discovered new varieties of plants and birds in the Southwest and in Mexico. His most lasting monument is his book.

Since they gave him back his life, it should not surprise us that Gregg all but worshiped the prairies. He writes of them in *Commerce on the Prairies:*

> Those who have lived pent up in our large cities know but little of the broad, unembarrassed freedom of the Great Western Prairies. Viewing them from a snug fireside, they seem crowded with dangers, with labors and with sufferings; but once upon them, and these appear to vanish—they are soon forgotten.

Earlier in the same chapter he explains what he means by the "freedom" of the prairies:

> I have hardly known a man, who has ever become familiar with the kind of life which I have led for so many years, that has not relinquished it with regret.

There is more than one way of explaining this apparent incongruity. In the first place—the wild, unsettled and independent life of the Prairie trader, makes perfect freedom from nearly every kind of social dependence an absolute necessity of his being. He is in daily, nay, hourly exposure of his life and property, and in the habit of relying upon his own arm and his own gun for protection and support. Is he wronged? No court or jury is called to adjudicate upon his disputes or his abuses, save his own conscience; and no powers are invoked to redress them, save those with which the God of Nature has endowed him. He knows no government—no laws, save those of his own creation and adoption. He lives in no society which he must look up to or propitiate. The exchange of this untrammelled condition—this sovereign independence, for a life in civilization, where both his physical and moral freedom are invaded at every turn, by the complicated machinery of social institutions, is certainly likely to commend itself to but few,—not even to all those who have been educated to find their enjoyments in the arts and elegancies peculiar to civilized society;—as is evidenced by the frequent instances of men of letters, of refinement and of wealth, voluntarily abandoning society for a life upon the Prairies, or in the still more savage mountain wilds.

"That government is best which governs not at all," Henry David Thoreau would argue four years later before the Concord Lyceum. But Josiah Gregg was no Thoreau. His adoration of prairie life is sincere, but his reasons are personal, not philosophic, and whenever he attempts to explain himself philosophically his logic goes awry. That phrase "broad, unembarrassed freedom," for example. Later in his apologia Gregg says that prairie men prefer to stay on the unpopulated ranges because they cannot reconcile themselves to "the habits of civilized life":

A long absence from such society generally obliterates from their minds most of those common laws of social intercourse, which are so necessary to the man of the world. The awkwardness and the *gaucheries* which ignorance of their details so often involves, are very trying to all men of sensitive temperaments. Consequently, multitudes rush back to the Prairies, merely to escape those criticisms and that ridicule, which they know not how to disarm.

"Unembarrassed," then, is no metaphor: Gregg means it personally. Freedom from civilization is not, for Gregg, Thoreau's transcendental necessity. It is a loosened collar and muddy shoes, an ordinary country boy's distaste for the big city.

Again: Gregg, says a biographer, "detested meeting people and was unduly modest in the presence of his intellectual superiors" (whoever those might be, considering Gregg's accomplishments—college graduates, presumably, as Gregg was not). Perhaps Gregg's discomfort explains his choice of "men of letters, of refinement and wealth" as his sole example of the type of men who refused to give up the freedom of prairie life. Who could he mean? Most of the "men of letters" who wrote books about their prairie experiences only passed through—Francis Parkman, Washington Irving, Richard Burton, John Frémont. The example must be defensive, as that exaggerated "multitudes rush back" is defensive, and more than a little wistful, since Gregg is writing at this point from a Philadelphia boardinghouse.

The man was obsessed with details, as we might expect of a hypochondriac. John Bigelow, the journalist who helped Gregg prepare *Commerce on the Prairies* for publication, complains of him:

He had no notions of literary art and he knew it, but he was morbidly conscientious, and nothing would induce him to state anything that he did not positively know as if he did know it, or to overstate anything. . . . Then Gregg had about as little imagination as any man I ever knew. . . . He would not allow his version of a fact to be expanded or contracted a hair's-breadth, no matter what the artistic temptation, nor however unimportant the incident; he always had the critics of the plains before his eyes, and would sooner have broken up the plates and reprinted the whole book than have permitted the most trifling error to creep into his description of the loading of his mules or the marshaling of one of his caravans. . . .

Is this the same dyspeptic traveler who complains that *ignorance* of the "details" of "those common laws of social intercourse . . . so necessary to the man of the world" forces prairie men back to the wilds? Gregg loved details, collected details, broke down every experience into manageable details. An eye for details distinguishes *Commerce on the Prairies*. It is the very quality that has kept the book alive and in circulation for more than a hundred years. Yet he capitulates before the details of civilized life.

His anxiety must have been unbearable whenever he confronted civilization. It was, as we know. It sent him cowering to bed, a fester of symptoms. No wonder he insists that freedom is a necessity of prairie life. Not a feature, not a privilege: a necessity.

Civilization worried him even where his beloved prairie was concerned. He takes pains to make the wilderness polite, populating it with gentlemen, talking mysteriously of "the still more savage mountain wilds." He cannot admit how much the quite adequate wildness of the prairies means to him, though obliquely he does so in another illogical paragraph:

It will hardly be a matter of surprise then . . . that this
passion for Prairie life . . . will be very apt to lead me
upon the plains again, to spread my bed with the mustang and the buffalo, under the broad canopy of heaven,
—there to seek to maintain undisturbed my confidence
in men, by fraternizing with the little prairie dogs and
wild colts, and the still wilder Indians. . . .

How does a man maintain his "confidence in men" by fraternizing with animals? Does Gregg mean he is more confident
of men when he can view them from a distance? But that is
not what he says. Does he mean that what little confidence
he has he prefers to leave undisturbed? But that also is not
what he says.

He says fraternizing with prairie dogs and colts and Indians
maintains his confidence in men. *Nature,* as he would have
conceived it, nature unrestrained, as his own nature was inhibited. The necessity of freedom: to be natural, muddy
boots and all. Not by accident did Gregg consider the wild
mustang the most noble of beasts.

He came as near as he could to freedom from his symptoms while traveling the prairies, but that was none too near.
He followed a respectable trade. He kept the wilderness at a
distance by objectifying it, by studying it as a collection of
details rather than a complete experience. Yet he understood
without ever quite admitting it to himself that life—his life—
depended on the wildness, that he must ride toward the
squall line, the boiling thunderheads, not back toward the
cities of men.

Gregg himself confirms these assertions. He is writing what
amounts to a guidebook for prairie travelers, traders, settlers;
extolling the beauty, the wealth, the healthfulness, the variety of the prairies. Anyone reading *Commerce on the Prairies*
immediately itches to travel them himself, especially since

Gregg insists one soon forgets the dangers. And there is the excellent map he included in the book, the careful mileages between landmarks. Yet, at the end of his book, Gregg declares that this land which he has praised to the skies for its salutary effects on man is "chiefly uninhabitable." Even though its "unequalled pasturage" might "afford a sufficiency to graze cattle for the supply of all the United States." Its choicest valleys and river bottoms, especially—where homesteaders traditionally settle first—are "too isolated and remote to become the abodes of civilized man." As if Gregg had never seen a railroad, as if all of America had not once also been too remote.

Josiah Gregg is a triumph, a neurasthenic who found a neurasthenic's paradise, a land where he could be miraculously healed from sickness, a land where he could even escape, for an hour or two on a warm afternoon, his obsession with details, and happily watch the prairie dogs play. Who wouldn't nail up a NO TRESPASSING sign on such a paradise?

The heartland as hideout: it is a theme that recurs.

Henry Chatillon

HENRY CHATILLON APPEARS AND DISAPPEARS QUICKLY ENOUGH. He represents a type of man who belongs to the Midwestern past and should be noticed, the type represented also by Jim Bridger and Daniel Boone. Chatillon was Francis Parkman's guide during the expedition "of curiosity and amusement," as Parkman calls it, that resulted in Parkman's book *The Oregon Trail.*

Parkman and his Harvard classmate Quincy Adams Shaw have come out from Boston, both of them twenty-three years old and two years graduated, to make a tour of the prairie regions. They will follow Nebraska's Platte River to Fort Laramie, ride south along the eastern edge of the Black Hills to Pueblo, and follow the Arkansas River back to Westport Landing. They are both accomplished horsemen and fair shots, Parkman serious and sure of himself in any circumstance, Shaw lazier, with something like a sense of humor. Both are snobs, in a casual way, but the snobbery gives an edge to Parkman's characterizations that is entirely agreeable. There is a touch of condescension even in his first description of Henry Chatillon, but thereafter, in *The Oregon Trail*, he never refers to Henry without the respect the man deserves. This is Henry Chatillon, a portrait in lavender and iron:

On coming one afternoon to the [Fur Company office in St. Louis], we found there a tall and exceedingly well-dressed man, with a face so open and frank that it attracted our notice at once. We were surprised at being told that it was he who wished to guide us to the mountains. He was born in a little French town near St. Louis, and from the age of fifteen years had been constantly in the neighborhood of the Rocky Mountains, employed for the most part by the company, to supply their forts with buffalo meat. . . . He had arrived in St. Louis the day before, from the mountains, where he had been for four years; and he now asked only to go and spend a day with his mother, before setting out on another expedition. His age was about thirty; he was six feet high, and very powerfully and gracefully moulded. The prairies had been his school; he could neither read nor write, but he had a natural refinement and delicacy of mind, such as is rare even in women. His manly face was a mirror of uprightness, simplicity, and kindness of heart; he had, moreover, a keen perception of character, and a tact that would preserve him from flagrant error in any society.

21

Henry had not the restless energy of an Anglo-American. He was content to take things as he found them; and his chief fault arose from an excess of easy generosity, not conducive to thriving in the world. Yet it was commonly remarked of him, that whatever he might choose to do with what belonged to himself, the property of others was always safe in his hands. His bravery was as much celebrated in the mountains as his skill in hunting; but it is characteristic of him that in a country where the rifle is the chief arbiter between man and man, he was very seldom involved in quarrels. Once or twice, indeed, his quiet good nature had been mistaken and presumed upon, but the consequences of the error were such, that no one was ever known to repeat it. No better evidence of the intrepidity of his temper could be asked, than the common report he had killed more than thirty grizzly bears. He was proof of what unaided nature will sometimes do. I have never, in the city or in the wilderness, met a better man than my true-hearted friend, Henry Chatillon.

From St. Louis the party proceeds by steamboat on the Missouri River to Westport Landing (which is today part of Kansas City, Missouri) and from there west into Indian Territory across what is now eastern Kansas north to the Platte. The men meet Indians; hunt buffalo; explore the Black Hills; live in Indian camps, Parkman for a time alone. Parkman contracts malaria and suffers from the weakness of it for two months of the journey, but presses on regardless, though at times he is too weak to do much more than hold on to his saddle. The two races which are most obviously missing from the prairies today—the Indians and the buffalo—occupy much of Parkman's narrative, thronging, both races, with an excitement and confusion that seems a foreshadowing of

their end, as if they were performing for this Brahmin white man their final performance, colored and heightened perhaps by Parkman's febrile vision of them.

Chatillon is distinguished, in Parkman's narrative, by his frequent absences from it, yet one always feels his presence in the background, directing and easing the journey. He knows the land, the tribes, how to hunt, when to lie low. And each time he appears, the appearance has a quality of tact and good sense and profound feeling that leaves no doubt of the man's distinction.

His first words in the text are plain enough. The sky has darkened; the party has left Fort Leavenworth forty miles behind to the south; they are encamping for the night: " 'Drive down the tent-pickets hard,' said Henry Chatillon, 'it is going to blow.' " Blow it does, and rain with it, that night and for several afternoons thereafter, breaking up every morning to allow the tour to proceed.

Henry's next appearance is humorous, the kind of humor Gary Cooper embodied: "Henry Chatillon, before lying down, was looking about for signs of snakes, the only living things that he feared, and uttering various ejaculations of disgust at finding several suspicious-looking holes close to the cart." More Gary Cooper soon after: "Henry Chatillon still sat cross-legged, dallying with the remnant of his coffee, the beverage in universal use upon the prairie, and an especial favorite with him. He preferred it in its virgin flavor, unimpaired by sugar or cream; and on the present occasion it met his entire approval, being exceedingly strong, or, as he expressed it, 'right black.' " These are most of the personal details we learn of the man in the entire book. They are enough: Henry is human, Parkman has shown us that, human and completely at home in the wilds.

The buffalo, Parkman says much later, are Chatillon's book, but Chatillon must also have been Parkman's book, to his great benefit. Giving Parkman all due credit for courage and resourcefulness and intelligence, he could nevertheless not possibly have enjoyed so safe and satisfying a tour unless Henry were behind much of what he' did. He was too untutored in exploration, too green, to have done alone the things he did.

An aside: the major theme of *The Oregon Trail* is the journey itself, and the experiences Parkman encountered in the course of it, but a powerful minor plays through the text, evidence of Parkman's deep feelings for the natural world he is traversing: of the wildness of the wilderness, a wildness now forever lost. Standing guard somewhere in northeastern Kansas with his cook, Deslauriers, Parkman wakes from a doze to find Deslauriers alseep. Henry and Shaw, their turn at guard yet to come, are also sleeping, and Parkman realizes his isolation. Consistently, his best writing will describe this sensation:

> Far off, beyond the black outline of the prairie, there was a ruddy light, gradually increasing, like the glow of a conflagration; until at length the broad disk of the moon, blood-red, and vastly magnified by the vapors, rose slowly upon the darkness, flecked by one or two little clouds, and as the light poured over the gloomy plain, a fierce and stern howl, close at hand, seemed to greet it as an unwelcome intruder. There was something impressive and awful in the place and the hour, for I and the beasts were all that had consciousness for many a league around.

That isolation hardly exists today anywhere in America; it was where Henry Chatillon made his home.

It is difficult to say how aware Henry was of his impression on Parkman. A few touches—his well-fitted dark suit in St. Louis, the name he gives his horse, "Five Hundred Dollar," his personal neatness, his pride in his hunting skills—indicate that he was a more complex man than Parkman makes him seem, and undoubtedly he was, since Parkman's hero-worship must have softened his view of his guide. Yet Henry would have been curious about his wealthy Harvard boss too, and proud to be guiding him on so exceptional an expedition. It seems unlikely that the man would have left St. Louis two days after arriving there from four years in the Rockies for any less an assignment. So both men fared well from their bargain, and both seem to have come out the better for it. Parkman went on to become a skilled and influential historian, especially of the French settlement of Canada and the influence of the Jesuits there; Chatillon drops out of sight, but we can assume his appearance in so widely read a book as *The Oregon Trail* did his reputation no harm.

We catch other glimpses of Henry's quality. At Fort Laramie he receives word that his squaw, "a woman with whom he had been connected for years by the strongest ties which in that country exist between the sexes," is dying at a village a few days away. Says Parkman:

> Henry was anxious to see the woman before she died, and provide for the safety and support of his children, of whom he was extremely fond. To have refused him would have been an inhumanity.

Parkman and Shaw resolve to ride with Henry to the Indian village, but the night before their departure Parkman is struck down again with malaria, and must stay behind. The other two men go, and return short days later:

> At noon of the following day they came back, their horses looking none the better for the journey. Henry seemed dejected. The woman was dead, and his children must henceforward be exposed without a protector, to the hardships and vicissitudes of Indian life.

And then this quiet note:

> Even in the midst of his grief he had not forgotten his attachment to his *bourgeois* [meaning Parkman and Shaw], for he had procured among his Indian relatives two beautifully ornamented buffalo-robes, which he spread on the ground as a present to us. . . . It was some time before he entirely recovered from his dejection.

Parkman's is a skillful book, a valuable record because he brought exceptional literary abilities to its writing. He has the novelist's eye for significant details, and some skill at generalization, and Henry's intimate knowledge of prairie life to draw on, and his own country childhood as a guide. It is entirely an American story, though styled with a Boston accent. "No man is a philanthropist on the prairie," he writes in one place. Certainly, as his selfish account of Henry's Indian wife shows, Parkman was not. But who wasn't selfish at twenty-three?

Henry Chatillon as hunter: that is his finest role in Parkman's book. Here is his epiphany:

> When Shaw left me he had walked down for some distance under the river-bank to find another bull. At length he saw the plains covered with the host of buffalo, and soon after heard the crack of Henry's rifle. Ascending the bank, he crawled through the grass, which for a rod or two from the river was very high and rank. He had not crawled far before to his astonishment he saw Henry standing erect upon the prairie, almost surrounded by the buffalo. Henry was in his element. Quite unconscious that any one was looking at him, he stood at the full height of his tall figure, one hand resting upon his side, and the other arm leaning carelessly on the muzzle of his rifle. His eye was ranging over the singular assem-

blage around him. Now and then he would select such a cow as suited him, level his rifle, and shoot her dead; then quietly reloading, he would resume his former position. The buffalo seemed no more to regard his presence than if he were one of themselves; the bulls were bellowing and butting at each other, or rolling about in the dust. A group of buffalo would gather about the carcass of a dead cow, sniffing at her wounds; and sometimes they would come behind those that had not yet fallen, and endeavor to push them from the spot. Now and then some old bull would face towards Henry with an air of stupid amazement, but none seemed inclined to attack or fly from him. For some time Shaw lay among the grass, looking in surprise at this extraordinary sight; at length he crawled cautiously forward, and spoke in a low voice to Henry, who told him to rise and come on. Still the buffalo showed no signs of fear; they remained gathered about their dead companions. . . .

Henry knew all their peculiarities; he had studied them as a scholar studies his books, and derived quite as much pleasure from the occupation. The buffalo were a kind of companion to him, and, as he said, he never felt alone when they were about him. . . . Henry always seemed to think that he had a sort of prescriptive right to the buffalo, and to look upon them as something belonging to himself. Nothing excited his indignation so much as any wanton destruction committed among the cows, and in his view shooting a calf was a cardinal sin.

Henry allowed Parkman and Shaw to shoot all the bulls they wanted, because the bulls far outnumbered the cows, but he was a natural conservationist, and must have looked with horror on the slaughter that extinguished the buffalo in the 1860's, if he lived to see it.

The hunting scene is Henry's last appearance in the book except for Parkman's heartfelt parting from him in St. Louis, but it is enough. Men are not separate from their experiences, and it is safe to say that no more Henry Chatillons exist in America: his most powerful quality is his oneness with the natural world from which we are now cut off. It is useless to regret the loss of nature; it is impossible not to admire a man who knew no separation from it.

Even Parkman seems to understand the loss that will take place. Midway through his book he predicts the destruction of the Indians, though he overestimates how long it will take, placing it a hundred years in the future when in fact it took only another fifty to confine the last of them to narrow reservations. But looking back on his own last campfire, somewhere in southern Kansas, he captures his sense of foreboding in images of blackness and death. They are appropriate to an abandoned hunting camp, but they are appropriate also to the abandonment of hunting as a way of life, the only way the prairies knew until the farmers came. It is as if the clearing away of the buffalo and the clearing away of the Indian were merely part of the clearing of the land out there where no trees grew, and with that clearing came the disappearance of the kind of man Henry Chatillon was, and history began in the Middle West:

When we had advanced about a mile, Shaw missed a valuable hunting-knife, and turned back in search of it, thinking that he had left it at the camp. The day was dark and gloomy. The ashes of the fires were still smoking by the river side; the grass around them was trampled down by men and horses, and strewn with all the litter of a camp. Our departure had been a gathering signal to the birds and beasts of prey. Scores of wolves were prowling about the smouldering fires, while the multitudes were roaming over the neighboring prairie; they all fled as Shaw approached, some running over the sand-beds and some over the grassy plains. The vultures in great clouds were soaring overhead, and the dead bull near the camp was completely blackened by the flock that had alighted upon it; they flapped their broad wings and stretched upwards their crested heads and long skinny necks, fearing to remain, yet reluctant to leave their disgusting feast. As he searched about the fires he saw the wolves seated on the hills waiting for his departure. Having looked in vain for his knife, he mounted again, and left the wolves and the vultures to banquet undisturbed.

William Hornaday's Wonders

In the 1880's, the Smithsonian Institution woke up to discover that the vast herds of buffalo which had thronged the prairie West had disappeared. It sent out a man, William T. Hornaday, to attempt to locate any buffalo remaining alive. Excerpts from his report follow.

THE GEOGRAPHICAL CENTER OF THE GREAT SOUTHERN HERD [OF buffalo] during the few years of its separate existence previous to its destruction was very near the present site of Garden City, Kansas. On the east, even as late as 1872, thousands of buffaloes ranged within ten miles of Wichita, which was then the headquarters of a great number of buffalo-hunters, who plied their occupation vigorously during the winter. On the north the herd ranged within 25 miles of the Union Pacific, until the swarm of hunters coming down from the north drove them farther and farther south. On the west, a few small bands ranged as far as Pike's Peak and the South Park, but the main body ranged east of the town of Pueblo, Colorado. In the southwest, buffaloes were abundant as far as the Pecos and the Staked Plains, while the southern limit of the herd was about on a line with the southern boundary of New Mexico. . . .

During the years from 1866 to 1871, inclusive, the Atchison, Topeka and Santa Fe Railway, and what is now known as the Kansas Pacific, or Kansas division of the Union Pacific Railway, were constructed from the Missouri River westward across Kansas, and through the heart of the southern buffalo range. The southern herd was literally cut to pieces by the railways, and every portion of its range rendered easily accessible. There had always been a market for buffalo robes at a fair price, and as soon as the railways crossed the buffalo country the slaughter began. The rush to the range was only surpassed by the rush to the gold mines of California in earlier years. The railroad builders, teamsters, fortune-seekers, "professional" hunters, trappers, guides, and every one out of a job turned out to hunt buffalo for hides and meat. The merchants who had already settled in all the little towns along the three great railways saw an opportunity to make money out of the buffalo product, and forthwith began to organize and supply hunting-parties with arms, ammunition, and provisions, and send them to the range. An immense business of this kind was done by the merchants of Dodge City, Wichita, and Leavenworth, and scores of smaller towns did a corresponding amount of business in the same line. During the years 1871 to 1874 but little else was done in that country except buffalo killing. Central depots were established in the best buffalo country, from whence hunting parties operated in all directions. Buildings were erected for the curing of meat, and corrals were built in which to heap up the immense piles of buffalo skins that accumulated. . . .

At first the utmost wastefulness prevailed. Every one

wanted to kill buffalo, and no one was willing to do the skinning and curing. Thousands upon thousands of buffalo were killed for their tongues alone, and never skinned. Thousands more were wounded by unskillful marksmen and wandered off to die and become a total loss. . . .

The slaughter which began in 1871 was prosecuted with great vigor and enterprise in 1872, and reached its height in 1873. By that time, the country fairly swarmed with hunters, each party putting forth its utmost efforts to destroy more buffaloes than its rivals. By that time experience had taught the value of thorough organization, and the butchering was done in a more business-like way. By a coincidence that proved fatal to the bison, it was just at the beginning of the slaughter that breech-loading, long-range rifles attained what was practically perfection. . . . Before the leaden hail of thousands of these deadly breech-loaders the buffaloes went down at the rate of several thousands daily during the hunting season. . . .

Of course the slaughter was greatest along the lines of the three great railways—the Kansas Pacific, the Atchison, Topeka and Santa Fe, and the Union Pacific, about in the order named. It reached its height in the season of 1873. During that year the Atchison, Topeka and Santa Fe Railroad carried out of the buffalo country 251,443 robes, 1,617,000 pounds of meat, and 2,743,100 pounds of bones. The end of the southern herd was then near at hand. Could the southern buffalo range have been roofed over at that time it would have made one vast charnel-house. Putrefying carcasses, many of them with the hide still on, lay thickly scattered over thousands of square miles of the level prairie, poisoning the air and water and offending the sight. The remaining herds had become mere scattered bands, harried and driven hither and thither by the hunters, who now swarmed almost as thickly as the buffaloes. . . .

White hunters were not allowed to hunt the Indian Territory [defined at that time by the southern border of Kansas], and the southern boundary of the State of Kansas was picketed by them, and a herd no sooner crossed the line going north than it was destroyed. Every water-hole was guarded by a camp of hunters, and whenever a thirsty herd approached, it was promptly met by rifle-bullets. . . .

During this entire period the slaughter of buffaloes was universal. The man who desired buffalo meat for food almost invariably killed five times as many animals as he could utilize, and after cutting from each victim its very choicest parts —the *tongue alone*, possibly, or perhaps the hump and hind quarters, one or the other, or both—fully four-fifths of the really edible portion of the carcass would be left to the wolves. It was no uncommon thing for a man to bring in two barrels of salted buffalo tongues, without another pound of meat or a solitary robe. The tongues were purchased at 25 cents each, and sold in the markets farther east at 50 cents. . . .

Judging from all accounts, it is making a safe estimate to say that probably no fewer than fifty thousand buffaloes have been killed for their tongues alone, and the most of these are undoubtedly chargeable against white men, who ought to have known better. . . .

As a general thing, . . . the professional sportsmen who went out to have a buffalo hunt for the excitement of the chase and the trophies it yielded, nearly always found the bison so easy a victim and one whose capture brought so little glory to the hunter, that the chase was voted very disappointing, and soon abandoned in favor of nobler game. In those days there was no more to boast of in killing a buffalo than in the assassination of a Texas steer.

It was, then, the hide-hunters, white and red, but especially white, who wiped out the great southern herd in four short years. The prices received for hides varied considerably, according to circumstances, but for the green or undressed article it usually ranged from 50 cents for the skins of calves to $1.25 for those of adult animals in good condition. Such prices seem ridiculously small, but when it is remembered that, when buffaloes were plentiful, it was no uncommon thing for a hunter to kill from forty to sixty head in a day, it will readily be seen that the *chances* of making very handsome profits were sufficient to tempt hunters to make extraordinary exertions. Moreover, even when the buffaloes were nearly gone, the country was overrun with men who had nothing else to look to as a means of livelihood, and so, no matter whether the profits were great or small, so long as enough buffaloes remained to make it possible to get a living by their pursuit, they were hunted down with the most determined persistency and pertinacity. . . .

By the closing of the hunting season of 1875 the Great Southern herd had ceased to exist. As a body, it had been utterly annihilated. The main body of the survivors, numbering about ten thousand head, fled southwest, and dispersed through that great tract of wild, desolate, and inhospitable country stretching southward from the Cimarron country across the "Public Land Strip," the Pan-handle of Texas, and the Llano Estacado, or Staked Plain, to the Pecos River. A few small bands of stragglers maintained a precarious existence for a few years longer on the headwaters of the Republican River and in southwestern Nebraska near Ogalalla, where calves were caught alive as late as 1885. Wild buffaloes were seen in southwestern Kansas for the last time in 1886, and the two or three score of individuals still living in the Canadian River country of the Texas Pan-handle are the last wild survivors of the Great Southern herd.

The main body of the fugitives which survived the great slaughter of 1871–74 continued to attract hunters who were

33

very "hard up," who pursued them, often at the risk of their own lives, even into the terrible Llano Estacado. . . .

In 1880 buffalo hunting as a business ceased forever in the Southwest, and so far as can be ascertained, but one successful hunt for robes has been made in that region since that time. That occurred in the fall and winter of 1887, about 100 miles north of Tascosa, Texas. . . .

In 1886 about two hundred head survived, which number by the summer of 1887 had been reduced to one hundred, or less. In the hunting season of 1887–88 a ranchman named Lee Howard fitted out and led a strong party into the haunts of the survivors, and killed fifty-two of them. In May, 1888, Mr. C. J. Jones again visited this region for the purpose of capturing buffaloes alive. His party found, from first to last, thirty-seven buffaloes, of which they captured eighteen head, eleven adult cows and seven calves; the greatest feat ever accomplished in buffalo-hunting. It is highly probable that Mr. Jones and his men saw about all the buffaloes now living in the Pan-handle country, and it therefore seems quite certain that not over twenty-five individuals remain. These are so few, so remote, and so difficult to reach, it is to be hoped no one will consider them worth going after, and that they will be left to take care of themselves. . . .

Such was the end of the Great Southern herd. In 1871 it contained certainly no fewer than three million buffaloes; and by the beginning of 1875 its existence as a herd had utterly ceased, and nothing but scattered, fugitive bands remained.

From William T. Hornaday, "The Extermination of the American Bison, with a Sketch of Its Discovery and Life History," Smithsonian Report, 1887 (*Washington, 1889*).

Mollie

MOLLIE IS ONE WHO SETTLED THE MIDDLE WEST. SHE KEPT A journal. It begins in 1857, a week before she and her family, the Dorseys, leave Indianapolis for Nebraska Territory. It ends when she and her husband, "By" (for Byron) Sanford, settle permanently in a Denver suburb in 1866, after the Civil War.

She treated her journal with special care, believing it represented a vital period of her life. She preserved the little book for three decades after its close; in 1895 she recopied and edited it during a long convalescence, and willed it to her grandson. "While I do not *pose* as a heroine, I know that I have had peculiar trials and experiences, and perchance *some*thing I have said or done may be a help to my posterity, for trials and tribulations come to all." The University of Nebraska published Mollie's journal in 1959.

Only superficially does it chronicle Mollie's pioneering. Where Josiah Gregg looked, and looked, and recorded every remembered detail of his travels, Mollie listens: listens for the feelings within herself that might explain her own uniqueness. She senses the uniqueness, worries about it, hardly dares suggest even to her journal that it is there. Reading the journal, we know that it is.

"There is something fascinating in the thought of the opening up of a new life, a change so complete as this will be," Mollie writes while still in Indianapolis. The change *is* complete—the change in her way of life. Mollie changes hardly at all.

She was born to pioneer.

By train to St. Louis, by steamboat to Nebraska City. "We are called the 'happy family.' " "Capt. Barrows said our fam-

35

ily had made the trip more pleasant." Thus they disembark.
While Mollie's father looks for a homestead the family
makes do in a log house, "one small room and a three-
cornered kitchen directly across the street." Mr. Dorsey se-
cures the land, "160 acres . . . 30 miles from here, on the
'Little Nemaha.'" The Dorseys migrated early to Nebraska
Territory; they will have a log cabin in "Hazel Dell," their
homestead by the river. Later homesteaders will brave the
open plains and learn to make houses of sod.

With the cabin built, the family settled in, Mr. Dorsey
works in town, and much of the responsibility for the children and the home falls on Mollie, his oldest daughter. Mrs.
Dorsey came too late to the frontier; she can barely cope.

Sam, Mollie's brother, is bitten on the finger by a rattlesnake. Mollie and her mother successfully treat the poisoning
and Sam improves. "Poor Mother was perfectly prostrated
after the fright was over. She sometimes feels wicked to think
she is so far away from all help with her family. But it cannot
be helped now." Practical Mollie. "I am so thankful that I
am endowed with nerve and strength of character to help
take care of the family." She means it, without egotism. "Of
course I suffer from excitement as much as any of the rest,
but I seem to always know what to do, and have the nerve to
do it."

The nerve to do it. Mollie's strength. It worries her. She
associates it with a tendency to frivolity. Alone one evening,
she is "full of good resolves tonight to *do* better and *be* better
than ever before. . . .

I can sit here in the mellow evening's light, so still, so
quiet, and commune with the angel spirits that sometimes come to me. They seem to tell me in soft, sweet
whispers not to doubt, that this life, so full of cares and
perplexities, is not all. There is a life beyond this vale of

tears, and trials are but to prepare us for that life, where no sorrow comes.

I want to be *good*. I try to be, too, but some way, I fall into many grievous errors. Perhaps my light frivolous nature was given to me to help those differently constituted. I'll try to keep from going into any foolish excesses. May the sweet angels watch over me, and keep me in the memory of the vows I make tonight.

By "good," Mollie means "somber," serious, as she implies in this entry and in many others. She fears she laughs too much, finds humor in too many situations where others see none. A lawyer comes courting, his visit delayed by a brush with a rattlesnake. Describe it, Mollie asks—this is before Sam's accident, she has not seen a rattlesnake yet—and he falters before the word "tail." " 'On the end of its *tail*, Mr. Mann,' " blurts Mollie. " 'Yes!' he gasped, 'on the end of its t-a-i-l.' " "I might have said 'narrative,' " Mollie quips to her journal, "since he was too modest to use the more vulgar expression." But she was not.

One day the cow strays. The family "several days without milk," the boys having failed to locate the animal, Mollie decides to bring it home herself. "It occurred to me how much easier I could get through the tangled underbrush if I were a man! and without letting anyone know of my project, I slipped out into the back shed, and donned an old suit of Father's clothes, pulled on an old cap over my head and started on my pilgrimage."

She stumbles into a camp of men. "I could not scream nor faint as that feminine resource would certainly betray me, but thought 'discretion the better part of valor' and that 'he who runs away will live to fight another day,' and the way I travelled through those woods to the house was a caution."

Of her whirlwind entrance into the house: "It was very

funny to all but Mother, who fears I am losing all the dignity I ever possessed."

Mollie contends with the ideal of somberness that her religion would impose upon her. She worries that she is not fragile, as ladies are supposed to be. She wonders at her nerve. But there is more yet to her, the source of all her best qualities. A passion, a sensuality? The words are too blunt, yet it is something of both, a warmth, a deep openness to others and especially to her men.

One suspects it early in the journal, when Mollie has not yet met By, when she is settling with her family at Hazel Dell. She senses presences others do not:

> I have had a queer experience that I must relate. I had gone to bed one night, but could not sleep. My father was constantly in my mind. I seemed to feel that he was coming home, altho he had only left two days before, and his visits home only occur every two or three weeks, as it is so far, and he generally walks, as it is too expensive to hire a conveyance. So the idea of his coming directly back was too absurd for anything, but still the impression that he was coming, and would be with me soon was so strong that I finally got up and started a fire. It was not so cold, but I was shivering for some cause. Mother awakened and asked what on earth I was doing, and when I told her I was looking for Father, she thought I was losing my senses. Hardly aware of what I *was* doing, I ground and made some coffee. Mother was about to get up and shake me, when we heard the dogs bark, then voices, and soon Father was at the door. He was accompanied by Mr. Sanford and a Mr. Holden, whom they had brought out to get land.

"Mr. Holden is a spiritualist," Mollie concludes, "and readily accounted for it all by saying I was a 'medium.'" She is not ready for so glib an accounting. "I hope if I am to be controlled by any spirit, it will be for good"—that dutiful word again—"but I don't believe in spiritualism as I have heard it"—and in this disbelief the steady girl, the girl who almost always knows her own mind.

And the deeper Mollie, where is she? "Only I know I have strong impressions sometimes, something I hardly understand."

With these qualities Mollie contends, helping her family, working in town, being courted by Mr. Sanford for two years before she marries him (she refuses to marry until she is twenty-one). Only once in the entire journal does she have difficulty with her steadiness, though she and By cross western Nebraska at a bad season, though they struggle at mining in the gold regions around Denver, and By goes to war, and they lose their firstborn son, and a flood destroys their house, and grasshoppers drive them off their homestead.

Only once, on the occasion of their overland journey to Denver. Mollie and By will travel with Mr. and Mrs. Clark. Mrs. Clark, "Minnie," proves almost more than Mollie can handle.

Trouble begins before the trip:

> Mrs. Clark, who all along has been almost angelic, took a "tantrum" (her husband calls it). If this is a sample, I fear repetition of it. Then when we came home we invited her to stop at the house, but she preferred to stay in her tent, and said so many unkind things and made me feel so dependent, that we held a "council of war" and almost gave up going at all.

Minnie apologizes. The trip begins. *Friday, 17th:* "Minnie, Mrs. C., is improving." *Sunday, 26th:* " 'Minnie' has not spoken to me today. We were alone in the tent all this afternoon, so I have had plenty of time for meditation." *Friday,*

June 1st: "I walked 3 miles today and helped By drive the cattle, as 'Minnie' wanted Mr. Clark to ride with her. I wish I could walk *all* the way." *Monday week:* "Mr. Clark and Minnie had a quarrel. She threw herself into my arms and had hysterics. . . . I kept amiable, and succeeded in restoring peace, and tonight Clark is holding Minnie in his arms."

So it goes, to the end of the journey, when Mollie comments on it:

> This is my first experience at not getting along with anyone but I have heard that a trip like this would try one's friendship. Of course Mrs. Clark was only an acquaintance. I have always prided myself that I could adapt myself to *anyone*, but I have made a miserable failure. So many of the Nebraska people we have met have said, "*I* could have told you all about her disagreeableness," but I know she is not well. She makes me feel our dependence.

"She makes me feel our dependence"—it is Mollie's only insecurity.

We expect Mollie's journal to reveal the typical experience of women on the frontier. Instead it reveals—Mollie. She may have been unique among the women of her time, or she may not. She would be extraordinary today, or any day.

She was probably better educated and more intelligent than many of her contemporaries. She lived to a better standard; she and By's prospects were better. She stands out from the other women in her journal and in other journals; she exhibits a modern alertness and independence, joined, comfortably somehow, with the old deference and dependence on men.

Her passion remained in her, its object removed from her father to her husband. It is her most outstanding quality, the one she depends on for her mysterious strength.

40

In the Civil War, after By has been in battle and she has waited tense days, with the other wives, to hear who has survived, the word comes back that only single men were lost. Soon after, some of the volunteers decide to return home:

Today we have had news that a number of the 1st Regiment had resigned and were coming home, Col. Slough and Capt. Sanborn of our company. Now if our Capt. *has* resigned I fear By will not, and I am all used up. I have cried all day, and do not feel like writing. I feel like "one deserted."

. . . Last night while brooding over my troubles I had one of my impressions that By was coming home. As the names of Sanborn and Sanford often get mixed, I hoped it had this time, and sure enough! this morning the advance guard arrived, and as Col. Slough shook hands with me he said, "Let me congratulate you, Madam. You will soon see your husband." And so my dream came true, and I am happy in the anticipation of meeting him tonight.

By is late; Mollie has gone to bed. She hears his footsteps:

And now our life begins again, and if we have but little of this world's goods, I feel rich!! so rich!!

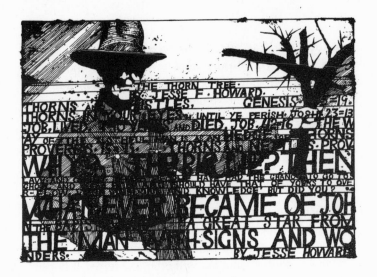

3 Fulton, Missouri: Signs and Wonders

EVERY PEOPLE DESERVES ITS GODS, AND EVERY COMMUNITY DE-
serves its achievements of fame and notoriety. The central
Missouri town of Fulton, with a state mental hospital to the
east, a Presbyterian men's college to the west, a defunct railroad terminal north and an A&W Root Beer stand south, has
achieved much. It is the "capital" of the Kingdom of Callaway, a sovereign state created momentarily during the Civil
War in the blundered truce agreement of a Union general. It
served as the Gothic source of Henry Bellamann's 1940 best-
selling novel *Kings Row*, a book subsequently converted into
a successful Hollywood movie. In 1946, Winston Churchill
delivered at Fulton's Westminster College his speech
"Sinews of Peace," in which he authorized, *ex cathedra* as it
were, recognition of the "Iron Curtain." More recently,

Westminster memorialized Churchill's visit by reconstructing on its campus an honest-to-Goshen eighteenth-century Christopher Wren chapel transported over stone by stone from London. It is a beautiful building, but, gods being gods, it looks totally out of place in Fulton.

Far from least in Fulton's Hall of Fame is Jesse Ernest "Outlaw" Howard, a spry octogenarian living out his final years among the ragweed and thorn trees up on Old Jeff City Hill, in the southwest corner of town.

Howard paints signs. The signs have messages on them which he composed himself, with narrow means that include a sixth-grade education, an old Webster's Dictionary, two daily newspapers, and a King James Bible. The messages are often cantankerous, usually argumentative, sometimes witty, occasionally wide with awe. They have not endeared Howard to Fulton. His seemingly pleasant retirement hobby has forced him to confront, painfully, the aesthetic, psychological, technical, and social realities of print culture. The price of that confrontation has been loneliness and some fear, but triumph too. Howard is behind the times by urban standards —us city folks are all post-literate, after a fashion—but he is a pioneer among his country neighbors.

He is, in fact, the Grandma Moses of print culture. Up on Hell's 20 Acres and the Suburbs of Hell, his two spreads on either side of Old Jeff City Road, you can see where it all began, all that daring, single-minded reduction of the rich evanescence of speech to the hard discrete permanence of print which made modern civilization and which now burdens it to distraction. And down in Fulton, so slowly do values change there, asking people about Jesse Howard means finding out what our forebears thought of print culture in the American heartland a hundred years ago. Howard is Fulton's pariah, a condition which charges his signs with an understandable bitterness:

SOME OF THESE FULTONITES
HAD BETTER TAKE A COURSE IN CIVILATION

Civilization, that is, or perhaps civilization and revelation together, an appropriate slip of the brush for a religious man.

He no longer posts his best signs at roadside. A spacious display of older signs can still be seen there, but his best work is stored away in thirteen handmade, locked sheds scattered around the acreage. Howard stopped posting signs because country crackers and Westminster fraternity pledges stole them as fast as he could nail them up. Someone threw a cherry bomb against the screen of his bedroom window one night when he was spying out a raid, making him fear for his eyes. A group of local purists even circulated a petition to have him committed to the state mental hospital, a place some Fultonians, Howard included, still call the State Lunatic Asylum, and fear accordingly. The petition failed, because his neighbors refused to sign it, but it made Jesse skittish and got him off on a quest by Greyhound to Washington, D.C., to see his Representative and ask for protection, a quest that ended shamefully when the Secret Service picked him up in the Capitol Building, put him in a wheelchair, delivered him back to the bus station and told him to go home. He did, and stayed, and despite numerous incidents of theft and harassment has continued the work that sets Washington and Fulton and even his own family against him.

"I ain't never got anywhere with any of this," he says with a sweep of a thick hand. "They just keep a-goin right on by. Right on by. I don't understand it. Never got anywhere. Got no cooperation a-tall."

It is a reasonable lament, but it expects too much of his community. The surprise of Outlaw Howard is that he got as far as he got in so short a time. Born in 1885, he did not begin making signs until about 1953, after a long life as an

44

itinerant worker, farmhand, and odd-job man. Since 1953 he has conceived and constructed hundreds of signs, painted several primitive paintings, invented his own version of manuscript illumination, drafted a long, entertaining chapter of nostalgic autobiography, and written fragments of a tragicomic epic about an eleven-year-old boy named Little Joe Cooper who hauls out his shotgun to defend his dog Tippie from the legalisms of a school principal and the dog pound. Howard may have accomplished more than this. He mentions a manuscript about John F. Kennedy, and other notebooks he has kept, but even in a week of visits to what he calls Sorehead Hill you can't see all his works.

"Jesse is only interested in making some money," a local official told me from the depths of a dark office, a Great Dane snoring at his feet. Of course a man who must live on his wife's Social Security check is interested in money. Howard has little idea of its value. He still talks about the plush times when he was making a dollar and a half a day. "I have a reputation that I am proud of," he wrote me several years ago. "I never sassed my father, or mother in my whole lifetime. I never was drunk. I never shot dice. I never played a gambling card for money. Don't know one card from another. Did use tobacco. But quit." Of what use is money to a man with no vices?

Jesse Howard hasn't, to Fulton's way of thinking, the credentials to be an artist. He must therefore be a promoter, or simply a madman. His "registry books" are full of the signatures of people from out of town who have stopped by to see his work. Their interest is something Fulton doesn't understand, and assumes to be patronizing. Thus Howard is a victim of cultural shock. Locals know he emerged from the same rural past as they, a way of life founded on a reserved, indirect verbal tradition. The public candor of his signs violates that reserve.

Howard's signs are a medium of their own, combining the

functions of newspaper headline, billboard, and town crier's ban. They link him with the literate world he discovers in newspapers and books, and because he is a primitive on the edge of that world, he believes the linkage magical. Speech requires feedback: so must print, goes Howard's logic. If public figures speak to him through the St. Louis *Post-Dispatch* and the Fulton *Sun-Gazette*, then he can speak to them in turn through his signs:

> MR. HARRY TRUEMAN YOU AND YOUR FRIEND MR. ADLAI STEVENSON ARE GREAT GLOBE TROTTERS. NOW I SUGGEST THAT YOU RACE HORSERS GET YOUR TROTTING HARNESS ON: AND TROTT TO EGYPT. AND MEET A MAN OVER THERE BY THE NAME OF NASSER. GO TO NEW YORK AND PICK UP MR. CELLER. MAYBE THE EGYPTIANS WILL GIVE A GOOD PRICE FOR

"Wonder what ole Harry Truman would say if he could see that sign," Howard said to me when he brought it out of a storage shed. Truman, a country boy himself, would probably be pleased. Down deep we are all equal. Most of the people whose names turn up on Howard's signs are pleased when they see one.

With few exceptions, Howard confines his sign-writing to public discussion. He reserves his private life for his notebooks unless a personal incident illustrates a public event:

> A MAN STOPPED AND WAS READING MY SIGNS. I ASKED HIM IN AND TO SIGN MY REGESTRY BOOK, WHICH HE DID, AND MAKE SOME REMARK ABOUT MY WORK, WHICH HE DID: HE SAID KEEP ON GIVEING THEM HELL" THEY= HAVE=IT=COMING.

LAW, AND COURT SHOULD BE CHOSEN FROM BOTH MEN AND WOMEN, WHO ARE HONEST. TRUTHFUL. HONOURABLE. AND LAST, BUT NOT LEAST, LOYALTY. YES, LOYAL TO YOUR FELLOW-MEN. BOTH, WHITE AND BLACK. YES, AND WHAT ABOUT BEING LOYAL TO OUR COUNTRY? AMERICA, THE NOBLE FREE AND AT ONE TIME THE GREATEST NATION IN THE WORLD. BY JESSE HOWARD.

I MIGHT BE A TOUGH OLD GUY. I NEVER PUT ON A UNIFORM, GUN AND A STAR, AND THEN GO OUT & BEAT A WOMAN UNTIL SHE LOST HER BABY. I NEVER PAID OUT $500 TO BE THROWN IN JAIL FOR. YET THEY THROWED ME IN ANYWAY. IF THEY CANNOT GET ANYTHING ON YOU THEY WILL FRAME IT. YOU DON'T KNOW THESE CROOKS LIKE I DO. I NEVER HAVE BEEN SUED FOR $30,000 HOMEBREKING. I NEVER MURDERED ANYBODY FOR MONEY OR DOPE. NEVER BURNED A NEGRO.

Yet among the jeremiads, occasional signs reveal his natural wit and lyricism:

WHAT EVER BECAME OF JOHN THE BAPTIST'S HEAD?

IN GOD WE TRUST
GOD BLESS THE OWL THAT PICKED THE FOWL
AND LEFT THE BONES FOR OLD MAN HOWARD.

> SOME PEOPLE SAY THERE IS NO GOD, ANSWER THIS
> ONE? THE COW, BLACK IN COLOR, THE FOOD SHE
> EATS IS GREEN GRASS, THE MILK SHE GIVES IS SNOW
> WHITE, THE MILK AFTER IT IS CHURNED INTO BUT-
> TER IS AS YELLOW AS GOLD, AND WHEN EATEN AS A
> FOOD IT IS GREAT NOURISHMENT FOR THE BODY.
> AND SOUL. BY JESSE HOWARD. THE MAN WITH SIGNS
> AND WONDERS.

And something beyond lyricism informs this Christmas sign, a heavy plank sawn in the shape of a star and wreathed with a string of colored lights:

A
GREAT
STAR FROM HEAVEN BURN-
ING AS IT WERE A LAMP,
AND THE NAME OF THE
STAR IS CALLED WORMWOOD.
MANY MEN HAVE DIED BECAUSE OF
THE BITTER WATERS OF WORMWOOD.
SEE REVELATIONS: A GREAT WON-
DER IN HEAVEN A WOMAN
AND UPON HER HEAD A
CROWN OF 12 STARS.

Kings Row, Henry Bellamann's 1940 novel, shocked Fulton as Jesse Howard's signs shock it, but flattered the town as well. Bellamann had credentials. "A lot of people talked about that book," one of Fulton's older citizens told me. "They thought they found themselves in it—they *hoped* they found themselves in it. Bellamann was a local boy, and a genius. Writing wasn't his real field. He was a musician. Director at Juilliard, professor at Vassar. His brother still lives here. He's a house painter, though he's old and sick now."

Henry Bellamann published five novels during his lifetime; his wife completed and published a sixth for him after his death. Two were set in Fulton. "The present volume," writes Mrs. Bellamann in her preface to the posthumous *Parris Mitchell of Kings Row*, "departs somewhat from its original purpose; it was to have been the psychoanalysis of the town as viewed and understood by Dr. Mitchell." Dr. Mitchell is Bellamann's alter ego in both Fulton novels, a young genius who grows up in turn-of-the-century Kings Row, leaves it for psychiatric training in Vienna, and returns to do his part in saving the town from itself. There is much that needs saving: a mad-scientist doctor who sleeps with his beautiful daughter, another doctor who is a sadistic religious fanatic and delights in practicing surgery without anesthesia on patients he believes have sinned, a latent-homosexual poet, a respected banker who absconds with half the town's savings, an evil politician, a prominent family with Negro blood. Bellamann divides good and evil as dogmatically as a Fulton preacher divides them on Sunday morning, and only his torrential, operatic sense of time and transformation saves him. A cracker chorus of feed-store loafers periodically sums up the action in *Kings Row*, after which noble young Parris Mitchell moves on to confront the next outrage. Hearty stuff, but tasting of pasteboard, like a store-bought pie.

Kings Row stimulated Jesse Howard's sign work. He owns a copy of Bellamann's novel, one of his few books. "*Kings Row*—that was wrote out in Fulton. We all know of this. You remember readin about a man got his leg cut off in a railroad accident? Well, the poor man's dead and gone now, but I have his peg leg."

THIS LEGG MADE OF WOOD IS THE REMAINS OF THE
MAN WHO HELPED TO WRITE THE BOOK, KINGS ROE.
AND THE MAN, WHO LOST HIS LEGG IN A RAILROAD
ACCIDENT, POOR OLD DOLL, WAS KICKED FROM PIL-
LAR TO POST. I HAVE HAD MANY CONVERSATIONS WITH THIS MAN.
THE LAST TIME I HEARD, THEY HAD HAULED THE MAN TO THE
S.L.A. AND HE DIED THERE.

S.L.A. means State Lunatic Asylum. The man's name, according to Howard, was Dahl Nevins—"Drake McHugh" in
Kings Row.

"He's got a brother here, livin here," says Jesse, referring
again to Bellamann. "I didn't know of the book. That's one
thing that kinda started me with this"—gesturing toward his
signs. "I didn't know there was such a book wrote. People
begun to tell me that they'd read *Kings Row*—that was one
reason why I started this thing out. Course you wouldn't rec-
ognize the places they speak of in *Kings Row*. And it's so
true—it just hits em. Now, all these old kings, what lived on
Kings Row at the time, they're dead. But there's another
bunch already come on."

The American Middle West is still a region of small towns,
towns permanently small. They do not grow; they only im-
perceptibly decline. "The town could lose more and more of
its blood," Parris Mitchell muses in *Kings Row*, "until it became as empty and dry as a locust shell. So many things, people—individuals and organizations—retain their form long
after life itself has withdrawn." Fulton is like that. It was a
town of kings once, if proud and energetic and ambitious
men are kings in America. Despite Howard's awe of the
town's moneyed leaders, Fulton's kings are no more.

Daniel Boone, in 1802, camped on what would become the
townsite of Fulton. The first railroad west of the Mississippi

was built early in the 1800's through the county of which Fulton is the seat. Lewis and Clark trekked across the southern edge of the county, along the Missouri River. The region came alive in the second decade of the nineteenth century when settlers arrived in considerable numbers from Virginia and Kentucky.

The site of Fulton was selected by James Moss and James McClellan of Boone County, and James Talbert of Montgomery County, who were appointed commissioners for that purpose by the [Missouri] General Assembly. They located the town July 29, 1825, and named it Volney after the French philosopher. The County Court on the first day of August following changed the name to Fulton in honor of Robert Fulton, inventor of the steamboat. . . .

The original town contained 147 lots, many of which sold for $1.00 apiece. The highest price paid was $56.00, and the proceeds from the sale of lots all together amounted to $1,946.18. The first lots were sold September 5, 1825. Edward G. Berry, who died in 1905 at the age of 97 years, carried a chain for the surveyor who laid out the town of Fulton. Mr. Berry was a son of Richard Berry of Kentucky who signed the bond of Thomas Lincoln when he was married to Nancy Hanks, mother of Abraham Lincoln.

This from a pamphlet, *The Kingdom of Callaway*, by local judge and sometime historian Hugh P. Williamson.

Callaway County sympathized with the South during the Civil War. After one long battle, Union General John B. Henderson negotiated a treaty with Confederate Colonel Jefferson F. Jones of Callaway, "the terms of which," says Williamson, "were that General Henderson, purporting to speak for the United States of America, agreed not to invade

Callaway County, and Colonel Jones, acting for Callaway County, agreed not to invade the United States of America. After this treaty, General Henderson retired with his troops. Callaway County, having thus dealt as an absolute equal with a sovereign power, became known as the Kingdom of Callaway, a designation which it has proudly borne and doubtless will for all time to come."

Jefferson Davis visited a county fair in Fulton in 1875, drawing large crowds. "Fulton has the warm friendliness of the Southern people who founded it," writes Williamson. That has not been the experience of all who live there, nor is it Howard's experience.

Bellamann decries the passing of Fulton's early leaders midway through *Kings Row*. Aging Colonel Skeffington, town lawyer and skeptic, whose family had traveled out from Virginia to settle the new region, sits in his office in the late afternoon and wonders what Missouri will become:

> The Colonel's old face sagged a little. He was disappointed in the whole damned state. They had lost sight of the thing that brought the best here in the first place. The unimportant people seemed to be conquering through sheer numbers. But even that might have aspects of hope if one saw anywhere among the young anything of those earlier qualities. They were little, they were downright picayune, they talked about money as if there were nothing else under God's heaven worth while. Their language was undignified and mean. They were not gentlemen. . . .
>
> Well—he shifted in his chair, settling himself deeper —he mustn't be too pessimistic. The poor qualities of the human race were always in evidence. One might as well believe in the enduring persistence of a few good qualities, too. These problems were no longer his. Others

would have to cope with them—but that was just the trouble—no one was coping. A new cheapness—a shoddy, sleazy social fabric was being accepted.

But . . . a shy feeling came from deep hiding in the heart of the old man . . . he loved this part of the country. He felt that it had been his country. He had helped it to grow. He wanted to see it do well.

At which point the Colonel dies quietly of heart failure.

Jesse Howard remembers another past, not of the small town but of the country around it. Memory makes heroes. A narrative of details is a narrative of magnification, and by it the flesh is made words, with all their enlarging mystery and power. In a fragment of autobiography buried among the wandering events of the *Little Joe Cooper* notebooks, Howard recalls his parents and their way of life:

"Now I will go back to the time when we used to have neighbours and friends. And when people lived in houses built with logs. And some of them, only dirt for a floor. And only a clapboard roof to shed the snow and the rain. And the boards were split out with a mallet and froe, and when they made stick and clay chimleys to carry out the smoke. And when Father and Mother were sitting in peace and quietness smoking their pipes, and they were made of clay. And, O yes, Father owned a small herd of sheep, and when we only had brush fences to turn our sheep and our cattle.

"And when a sheep would die, and especially in hot weather, Father would say, Jesse, that sheep has been dead for a couple of nights and days, and it is good and mellow by this time, go get a sack to put the wool in, and this sheep lay dead and didn't even move a foot whyle I picked the wool off of it's dead body, and one thing that I needed verry much, and that I didn't have. And that was a bottle of camphor. And that sheep lay dead, by the side of a big shed that used to house an old mill, and of, where people for miles around would shell turns of corn, throw it on a horse, and sometimes only a sheeps hide for a saddle. And off to the mill they would go, and as the miller only took out his toll, and that was a fifth for grinding, they would start out with a sack plum full of shelled corn, and come back with a sack plum full of meal. And, O my, O my, that good, good old crackling cornbread, sorghum lasses, ham meat and striped gravy. . . .

"And now I will go back to where I was pulling wool off of the dead sheep, and as I have said the sheep died by the side of the old mill shed, and of course the boiler required a lot of wood and water, and there was a large pond near by. And I use to stand on the old pond dam, and watch the old mother fish swimming around with her little brood of fish, and the man that owned the mill, his name was Gilbert, and a fine man was he, and he always kept poles, and fishooks, near by and whyle the people waited for their turn of corn to be ground into meal, the men and boys would grab a pole and line, and if they had good luck catching them, why they would take home a nice string of fish for supper or breakfast, and a plenty of good fresh corn meal, to fry their fish in too, yes what about those good old grayham muffins, with lots of butter and sorghum lasses.

"Well maybe you can stand another verse of scripture, and here it is—quote. Now David was the son of that Ephrathite of Bethlehem Judeah.= whose name was Jesse:= and he Jesse, had eight sons.= And the man went among men for an old man in the days of Saul.= First Samuel. Chapter, 17. and verse 12. page. 343=

"And now back to the sheep and the wool, and I had to help pick that wool over, and I will tell you how it happened, and why. There was no well at the house, our drinking water came from a spring, away down under a big hill, and as there was a plenty of water in the old mill pond, and it took a lot of water to wash that wool, we washed and washed it through some three or four times, and after it was washed, it was spred out in the sun to dry, and after it was dry, we would sit and pick and pick, until we got all the sticks and fine trash out of that wool. And at that time most every family had old time hand cards, which had little fine teeth, made of wire, and made, what they call rools, and they were only about a foot long, although there was a carding machine at that time, in Mexico, Mo. about the year 1890, that made rools about two feet in length, and Mexico, Mo. is some thirty miles away.

"And at that time Father had a spring wagon, and something like 200 head of sheep, and Father said to me, Jesse, I have a trip that we will have to make, and that is to Mexico, Mo., with some of our sheep, and we will have to drive them. So Father picked a moonlight night, and it was in the time of summer, and pretty hot, Father hitched his team to the spring wagon, and said, Jesse, go get the wool that we washed, and picked, and put it in the wagon, and we will take it to Mexico and have it carded into rools, and about three oclock in the afternoon, and after it begun to get cool in the evening we drove the sheep out into the road, and started on the way to Mexico, and it was quite a long journey for a little boy and the sheep, at about two oclock in the morning and we reached our destination at about five oclock in the morning, we had breakfast with a man by the name of Brown, and at his place, is where we left the sheep.

"BILL OF FARE AT THE HESKET BROWN HOUSE

"Pretty soon Mrs. Brown had breakfast ready, and a fine one at that, the bill of fare, was, ham meat and striped gravy, eggs, hot biscuit's with a plenty of butter, sorghum lasses, honey, and an assortment of jellys, and preserves, cream of wheat, ground with the old french burrs, and an assortment of all kinds of fruit, and their drink was, hot cofee, or tea, milk or water, and whyle we were in the house eating our fill, the horses were at the barn, filling theirselves with corn, oats, and hay, yes, Mr. and Mrs. Brown really possessed all of the good things that all good people should possess. And Mr. and Mrs. Brown's treatment was just the reverse, or opposite from the way that the scribes and the Phariseese and the Sadduseese, and the hypocrites, treated Jesus Christ, just before they drove nails through his hand's and nailed him to the cross of Calvaree, yes, Jesus was thirsty and when he asked for a drink of water, they gave him vinegar, to drink. And when he, Jesus, ask for some meat, they went out to, maybe a dead dog, and cut off a piece of liver, and was shure that they got the gall, and gave it to Jesus for meat. . . .

"And even after giveing, Jesus, vinegar to drink, and gall for his meat, they were not satisfied at that, and so they thought of even a more bitter dose than that, and so they add wormwood to the vinegar, and liver gall, the word wormwood, is what we call tobacco, and as I never went to high school or any kind of college, and I do not know whother it is a Greek word, or Lattin. And here is a verse out of the Bible, in the book of Lamentations that uses the word wormwood. Quote, Remembering mine affliction and my misery. The wormwood and the gall. Lamentations. Chapter. 3 and verse. 19. page. 848.

"And now since Mr. and Mrs. Brown had treated us so courteous and fine, both men and horses, got a good feed, and some rest, we hitched up the team, and over to the wool carding mill we went, and like all other mills, Father waited his turn at the carding mill, and my best recollection they had the wool carded into rools, at about two p.m. that day, and as Mr. and Mrs. Brown, lived just a little way's out of the town of Mexico, Mo. we stopped at their place to bid them good day. And on our journey toward home, which is near that great city of Calwood, Mo., in the city of Peth where one lives well, and the other two half starves to death, in other words they just barely exist, and as we drew near our place we called home, of which is four miles southeast of Calwood, and my best memory, it was about ten oclock that night, and there was a woman, looking, yes, standing in the door, and looking, for Father and I. And that woman that was standing in the door, and looking, yes, looking, was my dear loving Mother, and I am the fruit of her womb, and as I am writing this, with tears in my eyes, that I can hardly write, yes, I can see her dear loving face, as though it were only yesterday, yes, Mother, dear Mother, was full of fond affection, kindhearted, and true, with grace, mercy, love, and peace wrote all over her dear face, and never one cross and vulgar word did I ever hear, either, Father, or Mother, utter from their lips. . . .

"And, Father, yes, Father was a man that was small in statue, and always wore a beard, and I never seen Father without that beard. Father's name was Lawson Thomas, and he makes me think of the picture of Thomas, you know that old familiar picture that we see hanging on the wall of Christian homes. . . .

"Mothers name was Martha Elizabeth, and the mother of ten children. Four boys, and six girls, and five of us living yet today. Yes, Ettie, and Jesse, we are twins, and the youngest of them all and think of the task that father and mother stepped into when they both said I will. They were not like the two old katy dids sitting in a tree, one said to the other, Katy did, Katy didn't, Katy did, Katy didn't. Sleep all day long, go to bed early, and sing the same old sing song all night long. Man and wife cannot do this and expect to get along. Now I will go back to the sheep and the wool. The meat of the sheep is mighty good to eat, and is better than vinegar and gall. And the wool off of the sheep makes good warm clotheing, and it beats mosquieto bar, like some people wear today.

"Mother would say, Jesse go out to the barn and bring me

some nice clean shucks off of the corn, that she wanted to do some spinning today, and of course I never said no I won't go, for I always did as Father and Mother commanded me to do, and there was no sassing back, no, no, I knew better than that. I have seen Mother dampen the shucks, something like the women dampen their clothes before they iron. Mother would pick up a piece of the corn shuck, that I brought in, and wrap it around the spindle of the old spinning wheel, and then, she would pick up one of the cards of wool that Father and I brought in, and then she would give the big wheel a turn with her right hand, and you aught to see how fast that little spindle would go, and then with her left hand, she would reach out and pick up a card of pretty white wool, and then she would use the tip of her fingers to hold the card of wool to the shuck and in the spindle, of which was making hundreds of revolutions in a minuet, and the point of this little spindle is something like the point of a pitchfork tine, and by the side of old spinning wheel, Mother would walk, to and fro, and the point of this little spindle, would twist the card of wool into yarn, and after Mother had spun the card of wool into yarn, then she wound it on, what they called a broach, and the broach, was the same length of the little spindle, of which is about eight inches long, can you not see that the yarn, as it was spun was rapped around the corn-shuck, just like the thread is wound on a spool, and all of this was done at the same operation, and at the end of the day, Mother would have a big basket full of broaches. And it is hard to tell how far that mother had walked that day by the side of the old spinning wheel. And the next operation, was to pick up the broaches and wind the yarn into small ball's. And the next thing was the knitting needles, when Mother would sit up late at night and knit, and knit, until she had knitted two pairs of stockings for each one of the family. And the stockings that the women folks knitted in that day and age came away above their knees, now there is gloves to be knitted, and O, a dozen other things to do, babys crying, the geese to be picked, and I have seen the old gander reach around and almost bite a piece out of Mothers side, and there are the turkeys, Father and Mother would take them to Wellsville just a few days B.4 Xmas, and do their shopping, they would start early in the morning, and be late getting home that night, we children would go outside and look, and listen, yes, look and listen, and when we heard them coming, the older ones would go and meet them at the gate, for it was a long hard trip on them and the team, and in a day or two, Xmas would come, and there were nine stockings hanging on the wall, and gosh, they were big long ones too, we each one got something, some hard candy and a few nuts, or a harp, or a whistling bird, that would only cost a dime. No fussing, no grumbling, we each one got up early and with the biggest glee, and with that true Christ like spirit, and not only among our own household, that true Christ like spirit, at that time was with our friends and our neighbours, far and near, and how well I remember them running to greet each other with a merry Christmas, and a verry verry happy new year, and they would ask of each other's welfare, and how is everybody getting along, and this same Christ like spirit did not last only through the week of Christmas, why, it lasted the whole year through. And, O, that vow, which is only a three letter word, yes, that solom vow, that I myself took, when I took the wife to wed, and on new years morning, most every body would make a vow that they would live better lives and change their way of living, and some of them break that vow before the end of the week or month, and it would have been much better that they had never took that vow. Broken vows means broken homes, yes, broken homes.

"Good Neighbours, Days Passed and Gone

"Yes, we use to go to our neighbour and see about their welfare, and if that neighbour needed help, we would see that that neighbour got the help that he needed, I remember that there was a man in our old neighbourhood by the name of Hall, this man was sick and was in destitute circumstances, when Father went over there to see of their need's, Father came back home and hitched to the old spring-wagon, yes, the old spring-wagon that we used when we went to Mexico with the sheep, Father would tell each neighbour, of Mr. Hall's circumstances, and ask them to help this poor man out. Well you auto have seen the old wagon loaded down with every thing good to eat, there were all kind of canned fruit, sorghum mollases, meat, and potatoes, apples and pears pumpkin, and squarsh, cabbage, and beans, well, I do not know how much money that load of groceries would cost Mr. Hall today, and your guess would be as good as mine.

"And now it is getting time for some more scripture out of the Bible. And how many people are going out of their way to see about the welfare of their neighbour? And true fellowship and love, in Genesis. chapter. 43. and verse. 27. page 68. Quote. And he asked them of their welfare. And said. Is your father well. The old man of whom ye speak? Is he yet alive?

"And in that neighbourhood the family spent manny years of their life, I was only a boy of about eight years of age, when Father moved to the old mill site, and there is nothing left today, only the old pond dam, and, O, my, talk about good neighbours. And what fine times we use to have, and when the threshing machine would move in, there would be a plenty of help with their pitchforks and everything else that was needed to get the job done, they all worked, and worked with a will. And whyle the menfolks were out in the field, there would be all of the women in the whole neighbourhood, there helping to get a square meal, and talk about, ham meat and striped gravy, yellow legged chicken with dumplings, or dressing, beef roast, or mutton, O my, those hot biscuit, with all kind of jellies and preserves, and those fine cakes and pies, pass them around and say, which kind do you want, they always had a variety of manny kind. And their drinks were pretty much of the same variety, and that was not all that was gained at these big fine dinners and social workings. The young men had a chance to pick out a good cook. For what good would a wife be to a man if she could not even boil water without scorching it?

"And the young girls had a chance to pick out a good working man for a husband, they had the opportunity to look out in the field, and if they seen a young man useing the pitchfork for a prop, and maybe a bottle in his pocket, that young girl had better let that young man alone. Yes, these kind of people will bring gray hairs with sorrow to their grave. . . .

"Yes, fifteen and 20 years ago we had some neighbours. They were mighty fine men and women, and when we went to butcher our hogs, the neighbors were there just like the threshing of the grain. We sharpened our butcher knives to butcher hogs. And not butcher men. And it was a pleasure to work with these men, and these were neighbours that lived near the old mill pond, and talk about honour, manhood, and diety, these men and women had it. If a man's word is no good, neither is he, well there is always work to be done at a butchering, first thing to do is to put the kettles on some rock or in their frames with leggs, and next thing fill kettles with water and the next, build fire under the kettles, or vat, and then there is the platform to scald and scrape the hair off, and then there is the forks and pole to hang the hogs on after they are scalded and scraped, and the man most usually has all of this work done before his help arrives.

"Well I have the scalding barrel all set and the water it begins to boil, pretty soon the men will be popping up over the hill, and when they come, they most always bring their wives. And there is always a lot of work for the women folks to do, well here comes John Gray and Frona, John was always an early riser and he most always got there first, then comes Charley Noble, he married my sister Lena, and he was always an early riser too. Then here comes James Linton. We always called him Jim for short, well he was just the opposite for he was about 6 ft. 2, he was my fatherenlaw. For I finally married his daughter, and was a man that made friends anywhere he went, always jolly, always had a pleasant word to say, we lived neighbours for over 50 years and never a hard word between us. . . . Now here comes brother Dolph, and I do not see how that brother Dolph stood up and carried the burden that he did carry. It seemed as though he and his wife, Anna, and one daughter Gertrude, that their lives were all misfortion. Always jolly and jovil, their spirit with which they lived, is all that carried them through. They had no riches in silver and gold, all three are passed and gone, these people were rich in the eyes of God. . . ."

Good neighbors, days passed and gone . . . Kings today visit Fulton, but they do not claim its Kingdom. Winston Churchill arrived there on a windy March 5, 1946, to find 25,000 people waiting for him in a town where wags say the population numbers 10,000 souls only if you count the inmates at the state hospital. Churchill came to Fulton to deliver a message to the Western world, at Harry Truman's invitation.

The British statesman delivered "Sinews of Peace" at Westminster College. "It was one of the greatest speeches I ever listened to . . . and part of the policy of the Free World ever since," Truman said later. Churchill withheld his most important lines from the advance text, hoping the surprise of them would add emphasis. He knew how to coin a phrase. The cameramen, unfortunately, chose that moment to change film magazines. No motion picture of the scene survives. Only a recorder registered the key paragraph:

"From Stettin in the Baltic to Trieste in the Adriatic, an

iron curtain has descended across the continent. Behind that line lie all the capitals of the ancient states of Central and Eastern Europe. Warsaw, Berlin, Prague, Vienna, Budapest, Belgrade, Bucharest and Sofia, all those famous cities and the populations around them, lie in what I must call the Soviet sphere and all are subject in one form or another, not only to Soviet influence but to a very high and increasing measure of control from Moscow."

UNITED WE STAND LIKE THE SOLID ROCK GEBRAL-TA. ONE OF THE BEST FORTIFIED ROCK IN THE WORLD.	YES SEPARATED WE FALL APART. LIKE AN OLD WOODEN STAVE BARREL IN HOT DRY WEATHER.

"Mr. Churchill does not contemplate any other public engagements in the United States at the present time," a press release said. He came from England to Fulton and returned home.

In Churchill's place, in the mid-1960's, as if his iron words had been planted and had sprouted Portland stone, grew St. Mary Aldermanbury, a London church burned out in World War II and subsequently scheduled for demolition. *Pravda,* perhaps alerted to the existence of Fulton by Churchill's visit two decades earlier, disdainfully acknowledged the transfer, cementing for Fulton yet another connection with the entire known universe:

What attracted the Fultonians in St. Mary? Maybe the fact that within its walls some time ago the great poet John Milton was married. But maybe something else: here is buried Judge George Jeffreys, who sent hundreds of people to prison. Or finally perhaps because in the Court of the Church are buried the friends and associ-

63

ates of Shakespeare—the actors Heminge and Condell, the editors of the famous first editions of Shakespearean plays—"The First Folio." The only copy of this Folio was sold long ago to the United States. One way or another, cash on the barrelhead, and the stones are going to Fulton. Now it is up to you to figure out if the Chicago slaughterhouse kings take a fancy to St. Paul's—and yet you say this cannot be.

Pravda has its fancies too, and cannot see the fancy of two proud peoples interchanging their pasts.

Shippers mixed up the numbered stones on the way over from London, leaving the master mason, a man from Columbia, Missouri, a gigantic puzzle to work, but the chapel went up in good time. St. Mary Aldermanbury sits on an ugly base of modern stone like the base of a monumental paperweight, but that is its only fault. Christopher Wren, the English architect and mathematician, designed it among fifty-three churches he planned, between 1667 and 1711, to replace those destroyed in London's Great Fire of 1666. The steps in its bell tower date from the eleventh century. St. Mary Aldermanbury is symmetrical, spare, a pleasantly subdued structure supported inside by twelve Corinthian columns, lighted through large circular windows, decorated outside with stone carving and pediment-surmounted entrances. Elaborately carved lyres frame its large east window. The chapel contrasts painfully with the Steamboat Gothic town: despite its age, Fulton no more than the rest of America was built to last.

The paperweight base of the chapel is a museum filled with oddities of Churchilliana. Admission was free when it first opened, but vandals broke out expensive handmade windowpanes in the chapel upstairs, stuffed paper down the public toilets, and stained the museum's white interior walls. Now admission costs fifty cents, which pays for daily upkeep but is an irritation to Fultonians, who expected to come and go freely through a chapel they already think of as their own.

Patrick Horsbrugh, professor of architecture at Notre Dame and one of the Churchill Memorial Foundation's original consultants, described in a 1964 speech the connections he saw between Fulton, Missouri, and the rest of the world: "I ask you to consider, ladies and gentlemen, this extraordinary phenomenon of unrelated ideas and events that are now so directly linked together; a thriving college, a century old; a spirited man, mighty at the moment of distraction; a near-prophetic speech, derided at the time; the foresight to compound these factors; a memorial to needle-eye the past towards the future; a church by Wren, transported; the old made new to serve again its ancient purpose, now to stand rededicated, chipped and scarred as a constant declaration that, under God, human tyranny shall be defied." That reads like a worthy Shakespearean epilogue, and perhaps, as history comes to a close in the Kingdom of Callaway, it is.

Jesse Howard has built too, not in the high style of Christopher Wren but in the vernacular tradition of the frontier. He is a surviving example of one who works with what John A. Kouwenhoven has called, in *Made in America*, "the frequently crude but vigorous forms in which the natural creative instinct sought to pattern the new environment." Howard uses discarded materials, because his sensibility was shaped at a time when scarcity decreed that nothing be junk until it fell apart, and sometimes not even then. What others in Fulton throw out, Howard collects and puts to new use.

He has mounted the sturdy, simple door handles of old automobiles on the doors of his many weathered sheds. The front of an ancient Bendix automatic washing machine, freshened with aluminum paint, becomes the window of a new shed he has built, admitting light through its round porthole. A model airplane the size of a small tricycle, nailed together out of slats and turnings of broken furniture, decorates a mount of signs a car's length off the road amid green pasture. An entrance improbably located at the corner of a shed solves the corner with a gothic arch framed around the pointed door. Another shed is windowed with the flat, thick glass of an old Ford windshield, and the bottom edge of the windshield, a graceful convex curve shaped to fit the rounded hood of the old car, meets planking Howard has shaped with equal grace. The chromed front of a car radio, knobs intact, hangs nailed to the wall outside one shed. Green glass insulators from a telephone pole hang on another, and ceramic red roses on another, pure decoration. Commissioned by a neighbor to paint a dedicatory message on the wooden door of the neighbor's new doghouse, Howard responds with a selection of doggie biblical quotations:

—DOG. CHILDRENS BREAD CAST TO DOG'S. ST. MATTHEW, 15=26. PAGE. 997.
—DOG. CAST TO DOG'S. ST. MARK. 7=27. PAGE. 1026.
—DOG. DOGS, UNDER TABLE. ST. MARK. 7=28. PAGE. 1026.
—DOG. THE POWER OF DOG'S. PSALMS. 22=20. PAGE. 620.
—DOG. THE DOG'S COMPASSED ME. PSALMS. 22=16. PAGE. 620.

Serendipity is the essence of the vernacular. In Howard's hands an icebox becomes a rat-proof filing cabinet for his newspaper clippings and notebooks. Planking from razed houses becomes canvas for his signs and raw material for his storage sheds. A sheet of masonite and two buckets he converts to a bench under a comfortable shade tree. He uses fragments of colored glass to make clerestory windows over the door of a shed.

His paintings have the comic freshness of vernacular art.

Most depict animals, burlesques of human virtue and vice: owls, fish, skunks. As at Lascaux, the fish appear in X-ray views, fish inside of fish watching fish eating fish, a witty commentary on the natural world. The skunks appropriately illustrate a sign comparing their qualities to those of judges and lawyers. Other fish, with silver dimes glued to their mouths, are painted on raw shoe soles, Howard's own combination of sight gag, biblical incident, and Christian symbol.

In his notebooks he has revived manuscript illumination, spelling out words in block capitals with red and blue pencil alternating. An early page in the *Little Joe Cooper* notebooks shows a gourd vine, the vine in green, the gourds worked in gold paint, with this text:

THIS GOURD VINE REPRESENTS THE SHADOW OVER JONAH'S HEAD. QUOTE, AND THE LORD GOD PRE-PARED A GOURD. AND MADE IT TO COME UP OVER JONAH, THAT IT MIGHT BE A SHADOW OVER HIS HEAD. TO DELIVER HIM FROM HIS GRIEF. SO JONAH WAS EXCEEDINGLY GLAD OF THE GOURD. JONAH. 4TH CHAPTER, AND VERSE 6, PAGE 949.

On the same page, below, the vine is painted gold, its gourds missing. A green worm with seven legs, twin horns, and a baleful green eye gnaws at its roots:

THIS REPRESENTS THE WITHERED GOURD VINE, QUOTE, BUT GOD PREPARED A WORM, WHEN THE MORNING ROSE THE NEXT DAY, AND IT SMOTE THE GOURD THAT IT WITHERED. JONAH. 4TH CHAPTER AND VERSE 7. PAGE 949.

Following Howard around Sorehead Hill on a summer day to see his constructions and writings, I sweat in the heat and swelter in the sheds. He sweats not at all. Liver spots mark his temples, temples high beneath gray hair cut back at the sides like a soldier's, a spread of white stubble on his cheeks. He is a short man, with a ski-tip nose, eyes blue but clouded as if by cataracts, thick workman thumbs and fingers, hands that can wonder over individual kernels of the strawberry popcorn he raises, surprisingly dexterous in their care for small things. He wears ancient bib overalls, a rawhide watch fob looped through its special buttonhole on the top edge of the bib, blue work shirt open at the collar but with sleeves rolled down and buttoned even in the heat. His skin is weathered, leathery, his laughter surprisingly youthful, with an edge of shyness to it.

Once he traveled the western United States, a tour that ended in 1905 which he remembers so well today that in telling his life story he spends more than an hour on the working tour and passes over fifty years of marriage and parenthood in a few sentences.

It is a narrative of jobs, mostly farm work: shucking corn, threshing wheat, milking cows, digging potatoes, putting up hay. Only a few events stand out, and those are the "wonders" he means by the phrase he repeats again and again about his work and the world, "signs and wonders."

One wonder was an ocean-going ship in Cosmopolis, Washington:

"Great big old ship standin there on the docks. They'd been loadin that old ship a week or ten days, with lumber. I was always the dickins of a man to get out and look around, see what I could see. Loadin that old ship, every way, puttin it on there with derricks, horse carts 'n everything. Finally got the old ship loaded. I got up there on that old ship, you know, I didn't know anything about it. Had an old tugboat down the river, swiftest river I ever seen. Purty soon I seen that old tugboat had a rope up to that big ship, course the biggest part of it was clear under the water, purty soon I noticed the old big ship leavin the dock. I run as hard as I could run, and just made a daggone bee from there, off on the old dock. Three minutes, y'know, I'da been out there on that old big ship."

Where was it going?

"Australia! All that kept me from goin was that I didn't like those foreign languages. Lots of foreigners on the ship. The only thing that saved me was my legs. My legs has saved me several times from pickles."

The wonder of the ship, the mingled fear and delight at the idea of shipping out to distant ports, the anxiety over foreign languages—all these emotions are part of Howard's work today. In San Francisco he visited Chinatown and was told by his guide that some of the Chinese there ate tiger meat in the belief that it made them strong. It was a tale of horror he never forgot. It reappears on several of his signs, sixty years later:

FULTON, MO. MARCH 6. 1967. QUOTE. AN EAST GERMAN DOCTOR WHO SPENT 30 YEARS IN RED CHINA SUS-PECTS MAO TSE-TUNG IS SUFFERING FROM HARDEN-ING OF ARTERIES OF THE BRAIN. DR. ERIC BONDE-LEE, SAID, THIS WOULD EXPLAIN WHAT HE CALLS MAO'S UNCONTROLLED BEHAVIOR. YES, AND EATING TIGER MEAT. AND DRINKING THEIR BLOOD TO MAKE THEM VISCIOUS. YES, THESE PEOPLE ARE FOOLS, FOR WANT OF WISDOM. PROV. 10=21. YES, MAO TSE-TUNG HAS SUFFERED ALL HIS LIFE. FOR

Jesse Howard is an enthusiast. Except for the harassment that follows from Fulton's disapproval, he has no trouble en-joying life. Fulton is another matter—not thriving, not dying, suspended between. As with many country towns in the Middle West, its coherence failed at the end of the First World War. Its older citizens look back to that coherence with nostalgia, and find little in modern life that they can value. Its young people leave town, by the day or forever. A life of sorts goes on at drive-ins and taverns, as it always has, but it is a life that appalls. The few institutions in Fulton that prosper—the college, the hospital—look beyond the town. Only its merchants talk Fulton up, and they confine their expressions of allegiance to billboards out on highway 54, to garish new trash containers posted on street corners, to new store fronts faced with dusty plate glass.

Whatever Fulton's sources might be, old or new—and Jesse Howard is one of them as surely as is St. Mary Aldermanbury—they have not been tapped, despite the fact that small-town life is more intimate than city life and more permeable, and offers great potential for beauty. It is as if the entire town were waiting for the modern age to end. Meanwhile, the population slowly drains from the heartland's rural counties. The churches settle on their lots like ancient tombs, patient for Sunday morning. Variety stores sell Ouija boards. Cards in the windows of doctors' offices and drugstores announce county-wide revival meetings and promise healing by faith alone. Old men roam the town squares.

"It is just like this," writes Howard in one of his *Little Joe Cooper* digressions, "I ask a man 85 years old, I will only use his initials, and they are C.C. and I have known him most all of my life, we were standing on the street corner, and the thought came to me to ask him, this question, I said to C.C., if you had your life to live over, would you make any changes? And his answer was this, I would not want to live my life over. And the conversation stopped at that. And I see this man on the street most every day. And I asked an elderly lady, the same question, her age was 92, and her answer was this, yes I would. Now you might think that this is a verry inquisitive old man, well, well, that is where I get a lot of wisdom and knowledge, of which, we never get too old to learn. . . ."

Jesse Howard, reinventing the past up there among the ragweed and thorn trees on Sorehead Hill, is not too old to learn, but Fulton may be. Why else would a town so veined with the sources of the world beyond its walk continue to turn only inward?

IS THERE ANY LOVE IN THIS TOWN TODAY? GRACE. HOPE. FAITH. LOYALTY. DEITY. MANHOOD. CONFIDENCE. WHO CAN YOU PUT CONFIDENCE IN TODAY? I HAVE HAD A GREAT NUMBER OF PEOPLE TO GO AWAY FROM THIS PLACE WITH DECEIT & LIES WROTE ALL OVER THEIR FACE. 4 OF THESE ARE WOLVES & IS IT POSSIBLE TO FALL FROM GRACE LIKE THAT. GOD SAYS HE WILL STRIP US NAKED AND UNCOVER OUR SHAME.

4 *Harry's Last Hurrah*

INDEPENDENCE, MISSOURI, ON A SUNDAY MORNING IN LATE spring, breathes the quiet of a country town, birds twittering resentfully at church bells, the people, at eleven o'clock, gathered together for worship, and only an occasional car, rusting at its fenders, passing on the streets, aprowl for a Seven-Eleven store that might offer up its blessing of eggs and Alka-Seltzer. The Baptist Book Store is closed; the courthouse on the square that Harry Truman rebuilt is deserted; Denton Drug Store is dark except for its dusty windows, where apothecary jars glow with colored waters of no medicinal virtue; the offices of the *Independence Examiner* are locked tight against any news of the outside world.

Dr. Billy G. Hurt will preach at the First Baptist Church, a block north of the Independence Memorial Hall, where, as a teen-ager, I danced folk dances with dirndled girls. Where I later registered for the draft. The First Baptist Church service has begun when I arrive, and an usher with graying, close-cropped hair points me to a row of dark plywood seats tucked back under the balcony. After a suitably discreet pause, the elderly lady next to me passes a hymnal in time for me to turn to hymn number 487, "My Country, 'Tis of Thee." It is Memorial Day.

Dr. Billy G. Hurt wears the dark suit, white shirt, and white tie made familiar by another Baptist, Billy Graham. A pride of Billys in that denomination. Dr. Billy's delivery—his subject is "The Christian's Memorial Day"—borders on elegance. He has been to school, and knows how to use his intellectual weapons without snobbery. "There is a demonic force loose in the world," he says, "call it the Devil or call it what you will." It rolled itself up to overwhelm the world at Christ's crucifixion, he says. "Our young men have died in numberless wars in numberless places, and where is that better day their sacrifice was to bring?" Dr. Billy's jowl is heavier on his right side than on his left, and he juts his head to the right as he speaks to protect that heavy jowl from scorn, his hands white at the knuckles twisting the pulpit as if he would wrench it from the floor to dramatize his point. "In these perilous times there are not many evidences that God's love is stronger than man's hatred"—surprising sentiment from a Baptist preacher in Independence, Missouri. "The Christian's Memorial Day"—does he mean Easter?—"is better." It is a somber sermon, a surprising conversion of the Baptists' traditional hellfire and damnation into a modern idiom. Dr. Billy G. Hurt hurts, and his congregation, composed of the very young and the very old, listens, or seems to, the members of the choir in their glossy purple robes lined up behind the preacher especially intent since they are on public display, their faces fixed and stern. A Wollensak tape recorder, looking like a small air-conditioner, wheels silently atop a filing cabinet tucked into a corner of the wall next to me, preserv-

73

ing Dr. Billy for future generations of Baptists. The sermon sounds anti-war, the last thing I would have expected to hear in Independence, but the anti-war tone turns martial at the end when Dr. Billy proves unable to resist a metaphoric moral: "Christ's message to us is—keep up the fight!"

After the sermon, Dr. Billy welcomes a family recently moved to Independence from Kansas City, "Brother and Mrs. Calvin Strange," and we sing "Pass Me By" in ambivalent welcome—"I hope the Savior won't pass me by." As the Postlude plays its response to Dr. Billy's benediction, the lady next to me does her duty and satisfies her curiosity, welcomes me to her church, asks me who I am. Did President Truman ever worship here, I ask her in return. No, he was a Baptist, but he always went out to Grandview, where his family lived, to the Baptist church there. When he was in Independence he worshipped with Bess at the Episcopal Church. Her church. Where, I discover later, Clifton Daniel of *The New York Times* and Margaret Truman, only child of Harry and Bess Truman, were wed. The lady introduces me to my usher, who looks at me noncommittally and shakes my hand. The line passing Dr. Billy is long; I leave by a side door.

Independence knows its age, as few American towns can. Founded in 1827, chartered in 1849, it settles today rotting in its history. Its very name praises the victory of that earlier Revolution. It was the watering hole of the westward movement well before Kansas City clambered up the Missouri River bluffs. Here rested pioneers heading for Oregon and California: Joseph Smith and his fanatic Mormon band; traders outfitting for Santa Fe; and later, petty criminals that we celebrate as outlaws of the West.

Independence had little enough to recommend it: no adjacent river, no prominent grove of trees, no dramatic elevation above the surrounding land. But it had a spring, pouring blue water into the big brick standpipe the town's founders caused to be built around it. The standpipe remains; above the wet mud at its bottom now is posted a sign: WATER UNSAFE TO DRINK. That is what has become of Independence. Kansas City, cleverly snaking out annexation lines around the older town, has completely surrounded it. The young people have moved out to their little 50′ by 50′ imitation farms in the suburbs to fight crabgrass and sod webworms as their fore-fathers fought locusts and Indians, driving their camper trucks off into what is left of God's country on Sunday morn-ing when they ought to be in church listening to Dr. Billy G. Hurt keep up the fight. Except to the very old, Independence is no longer a town at all, but a cross-over point between shopping centers. Wild Woody's Bargain Barn looms up just down the road. Wild Woody may be more in the spirit of the old Independence than the camper-trucked young who pas-ture around it: he is fervently Early American, his full-page newspaper ads with a banner titled WILD WOODY SEZ and below that a new pamphleteering slogan each week in krazily-spelled dialect.

Independence was different when I lived there, on the farm at the town's edge—the city limits divided one of our pas-tures—during the years of Truman's Presidency. The town could not then have been more Midwestern as my adoles-cence meant the word, rural and shaded and slow, withdrawn behind closed windows and cautious minds. Preacher Bob, at the Watson Memorial Methodist Church (which is gone now, torn down to make way for the Stake of Calvary Center of the Reorganized Church of the Latter-Day Saints), deliv-ered more than twenty sermons on the books of the Old Testament, each sermon more boring than the last. Preacher Bob affected clerical robes, too, an ecclesiastical elegance that brought murmurings from some who preferred their Wesley-ism plain. Woody replaced him, a country man at heart, who met his name—it was really Woodruff—by carving a heavy

75

cross for Watson Memorial's chancel and rebuilding the interior of the parsonage. One summer a Methodist preacher in a nearby town was called up for enticing boys, and I shuddered to hear of it because he and I had talked late and lonely by a campfire once of my onanistic sins and my profound desire for Christian comfort, and I think he had his hand on my leg for Christ's sake. Next to the Memorial Hall in Independence rose another Methodist church, more fashionable, I learned from an Independence girl who attended it and later attended Radcliffe and ended up in Ethiopia. The two Methodist congregations had divided during the Civil War, Watson Memorial going Northern, the other church Southern.

Independence was that sort of town, too, though Preacher Bob made attempts at Christian charity. One Sunday he invited the pastor of the African Methodist Episcopal Church over—more murmurings—and once white missionaries recently from the Dark Continent told us of the horror with which their charges greeted a package of Aunt Jemima Pancake Mix, because the natives had become accustomed to finding inside America's packages whatever was illustrated on the cover. Or so I remember, but that may be a joke I read in *Reader's Digest*. It catches the missionary spirit, however.

And down the street from the Watson Memorial Methodist Church, a short block away, where I now walked after leaving the Reverend Hurt's establishment, sat Truman's high, elderly house. Not really Truman's but Bess's, given to the couple on their wedding day, because the grandmother of the bride wasn't at all sure that the new son-in-law would make good, though he was fresh from a captaincy in World War I and had $15,000 in assets in his pocket. Independence people still call it the Wallace house; it bequeaths a silence to the spaces around it stiller even than Independence on a Sunday morning, a silence forced partly by the stature of the house itself—a quaint elegance of white Gothic curtained against the poisonous sun—partly by the stature of its inhabitant. Mr. Truman was President Truman during most of the years I attended Watson Memorial. I used to walk down the block in the half-hour between Sunday school and church to look at the President's house. Inside the wrought-iron fence that surrounded the house's large lot, reflected from tree to tree by clever mirrors mounted in black boxes nailed to the trees themselves, a protective beam of light circled the house like Ariel circling Prospero. I could not imagine that any occupant of that house, any native or long-time resident of that town, could possibly be President of the United States. My hero of the time, because I hoped to be a missionary myself one day, was Albert Schweitzer, a man with doctorates at heavy German universities in music and theology and medicine, and with all that learning off in Africa treating natives. How could a mere Independence man who wore loud Hawaiian shirts be President? I would stand across the street from the Wallace house in hopes that he would emerge, and watch tourists take their pictures smiling out from in front of the wrought-iron gate. Truman never appeared. Even when he was in town, he apparently stayed indoors except in the cool of the early morning, when I was out on the farm doing chores.

His vigor, as Dean Acheson reports it in *Present at the Creation*, would have surprised me. Independence moved slowly, as one moves when very old. Old men sat on the white benches young Judge Harry Truman caused to be built around the town square; the few restaurants served the same heavy, ponderously eaten fried chicken and mashed potatoes and buttered peas and cream gravy for Sunday dinner that we were served at home. You drove slowly through Independence; the few stoplights barely turned. At the summer meetings of the Independence 4-H Club the discussion of dues

77

might run on through the entire evening. A President of
vigor and sprightliness? But listen to him:

> That summer of 1954 was abnormally hot in Kansas
> City [it was—the only time I can remember that we
> stopped haying at noon] and the thermometer outside
> the hospital windows [where Truman was recovering
> from surgery following a gall-bladder attack] ranged be-
> tween 110 and 114 by midafternoon. Mrs. Truman was
> at my side constantly, and she read the newspapers to
> me, as well as current magazines and many of the letters
> and messages that came in.
>
> I did not realize how punishing the heat was to the
> other patients and visitors to the hospital, which was
> without air conditioning. I do not mind the heat, and I
> have never cared for air conditioning for myself, prefer-
> ring fresh air no matter how hot or cold.
>
> When the director of the Research Hospital wanted
> to put in an air conditioner in my room I declined. . . .
> I felt that, despite the good intention of the hospital to
> provide me with every comfort, I should not be given
> special privileges, since no one else in the hospital was
> provided with air conditioning. . . .
>
> But several days later an old friend of mine . . . said,
> "It may be all right for you without air conditioning, but
> what about Mrs. Truman sitting here day after day in
> this insufferable heat? Why are you being so stubborn,
> and why don't you let the hospital put air conditioning
> in?"
>
> I sent for the hospital superintendent . . . and within
> the hour, an air conditioning unit was installed.

That is vigor, of a Midwestern kind. And pride, and a courtli-
ness that he made much of in his public life, though it has
always been difficult to visualize Bess as the cute, blond-

haired, blue-eyed girl of his dreams whom Harry often described.

So many of Truman's qualities came directly from his Midwestern past. His decisiveness. "He slept, so he told us," says Acheson, "as soon as his head touched the pillow, never worrying, because he could not stay awake long enough to do so." "With the President a decision made was done with and he went on to another"—Acheson again. Truman was called stubborn often enough. "Stubborn" is the pejorative of "decisive," and a physically small man, especially one so astigmatic as Harry, would learn stubbornness early in a small town if he had any gumption, and Harry did. He would be forever defending his stature, his weak eyes, his endless books, his rights in a knitted family that didn't always know the best of times, though it never knew the worst.

"My mother was partial to the boys," writes Truman in his *Memoirs*, "both in the family and in the neighborhood. I used to watch my father and mother closely to learn what I could do to please them, just as I did with my schoolteachers and playmates. Because of my efforts to get along with my associates I usually was able to get what I wanted. It was successful on the farm, in school, in the Army, and particularly in the Senate." It is the way the physically weaker but mentally more alert boy or man converts the stronger.

Imagine, then, Harry bantying around a battlefield, elated with his power to command for perhaps the first time in his life without subterfuge, yet learning awful lessons of the cost of his command in the lives of men he knew not only in battle but also back home. More than one historian has said Harry Truman was shaped there, in France, running a profitable commissary in his spare time with Eddie Jacobson (the same who would later help him near to bankruptcy and take that pledge himself) but facing, in the flaring darkness of battle, the cost of every decision he made.

And probably shrinking at first from such consequences, drawing the old stubbornness about himself for solace, yet gradually giving up the elation, clearing away the decision-making process until only the fact of the decision was left, until he knew that, whatever else it might cost him, a decision would not cost him his sanity or his self-respect; it would be made to the best of his knowledge and ability and he would then forget it: "He done his damndest," Harry's favorite epitaph.

One gives up squeamishness too in such a circumstance, as one gives it up on the farm, where after the war Harry spent twelve working years of his long life. Plowing makes way for sowing, and sowing for a solid field of wheat and tall corn; but the day comes when those sweated and nurtured crops must be cut and stored, or cut and sold, the grain to be fed to animals which in their turn will be slaughtered; and that is the way of the natural world, and you give up squeamishness or you subside. Truman then, and Truman as President, had no intention of subsiding.

Instead he became enamored of the process of making decisions, juvenated by the continual rediscovery that it was possible to make things happen, to move the world, to go from A to B to C and even all the way to Z by so simple and logical a procedure as making a decision. It became most of what he talked about and wrote about, and read about as well. He ranks Presidents by their ability to make important decisions, and he will himself be ranked high because he made some of the most important decisions of the century. My God, no wonder the man is stubborn. Though he has read as many books as any man alive, he never went to college; to discover that among the Achesons and the Cliffords, fair gentlemen from Yale and St. Louis, he need only listen to each man's information and opinion, test them against his encyclopedic knowledge of American history and his own good horse sense, and come up with the right decision more than half the time: that prided him beyond belief. Acheson ascribes Truman's perpetual cheerfulness to his healthy genealogy, but it came instead from his joy at being the man who gets to make more important decisions every day than any other on the face of the earth. He never doubted who he was, plain Harry Truman, a "great little man" as Acheson rather condescendingly puts it; but he never doubted, either, that he was possessed of a Jovian gift.

And for years after he left office, the people at the Truman Library say, political scientists came round asking Truman about his "decision-making process," and Truman laughed and scoffed and looked the other way. As far as he was concerned, it's the simplest thing in the world once you get the hang of it. "What was your most difficult decision?" the kids used to ask Harry when he spoke to them in the auditorium of the Library. "Korea. Korea," he'd say. "That was the most difficult decision, because that involved the whole free world. That was the most difficult decision to be made. And it saved Korea as a free government which had been set up by the United Nations, and the Republic of Korea was saved. But that was the hardest decision that had to be made because it involved the whole free world."

And the others? Dropping the atomic bomb? Joining the United Nations? Fighting John L. Lewis? The Marshall Plan? The Cold War? The campaign of 1948? The Berlin Airlift? Firing MacArthur? What on earth would the man have done with Vietnam?

After decisiveness, loyalty. Queer loyalty when it involved defending people like Harry Vaughan or showing up as President of the United States for Kansas City Boss Tom Pendergast's funeral. But remember also his loyalty to people like Acheson and Marshall. What else but loyalty from a battle commander, a 33rd-degree Mason, a man helped into office by Missouri's unregenerately partisan Democratic party? But what else also from a man who remembered, as a boy, a happy childhood full of pigeon-raising, wood-cutting, gardening, and small-town gangs? "At the corner of Delaware and Waldo, east of us [in Independence], were the Sawyers, the Wallaces, and the Thomases. Lock Sawyer was older than we were, and the Wallaces were a year or two younger. Bess, Frank, and George Wallace all belonged to the Waldo Avenue gang. Across the street at Woodland College were Paul and Helen Bryant. Paul and Vivian [Truman's brother] were great friends and raised pigeons and game chickens in partnership. We had wonderful times in that neighborhood from 1896 to 1902. Our house soon became headquarters for all the boys and girls around. . . ." What else for Truman but intense loyalties? It was how he grew up, how he lived his life. Acheson, who used to return to Yale to visit his old secret society, Scroll and Key, understood well enough, and so did Clark Clifford, that handsome, brilliant, discreet mother of Presidents. Truman's men began calling themselves "the old contemptibles"; Truman they called "the Chief"; and whatever their understanding of their group, for Truman it must have seemed some nationally convened neighborhood gang. He conducted the affairs of state—we have Acheson's word for this, though what follows is not his patrician image —as if they were discussions of what activities, what mischief or good deeds, should issue forth from the treehouse today, and Truman chief of the Treehouse Association.

Writes Acheson: "[Truman's was] a truly hospitable and generous mind, that is, a mind warm and welcoming in its reception of other people's ideas. Not in any sense self-deprecating, his approach was sturdy and self-confident, but without any trace of pretentiousness. He held his own ideas in abeyance until he had heard and weighed the ideas of others, alert and eager to gain additional knowledge and new

82

insights. He was not afraid of the competition of others' ideas; he welcomed it." It is not fanciful to imagine the mature Truman remembering, amid the affairs of state, the old gangs and how they worked; his worst word for the Nazis, and later for Stalin's bunch, was "gangsters," and to him that word means more than Ma Barker and Al Capone. Truman is fond of saying he is a cross between two of Missouri's other famous residents, Mark Twain and Jesse James. He may well be.

He was proud of the Marshall Plan, and it was his and Acheson's and Clark Clifford's more than General Marshall's; he was delighted with Point Four, the Peace Corps' predecessor, promising—as it did not fulfill—a sort of Midwestern chiropractic of international healing; he regretted Korea with a fierce unyielding regret born of battle in World War I; he was scared as hell of MacArthur, and immensely relieved when he removed that addled bully from his Japanese throne; he found Potsdam trying, but did his level best, and the odds were not favorable: "In a physical sense I found the [Potsdam] conference to be exacting. Churchill and Stalin were given to late hours, while I was an early riser. This made my days extra long. . . . I was glad to be on my way home." No country boy could hope to keep up with those two advanced alcoholics on their own terms. Truman moans the odd hour of their formal meetings—5:30 in the afternoon—but he stuck them out. He had known odd hours before.

Greatness as a President is not necessarily good, and it may very well be evil, depending on how you like what that greatness accomplished. Remember that this snappy dresser from Independence, this plain practical man, helped to construct the national and global politics of our present age. He invented the Cold War; he desegregated the Armed Forces and the civil service; he laid the groundwork, in his Korean "police action," for Vietnam; he backed NATO and the United

Nations; he confiscated the coal mines and would have confiscated the railroads to force the federal will: he took power from the other branches of government, as all strong Presidents do. And he did it all in the name of sweet reason, a name he believes. The irrational has no place in his canon, though even his neighbor Dr. Billy G. Hurt insists that the diabolic was loosed into the world long ago. And soon enough we will have to dismantle this age Truman created with the clever Dean and the subtle Clark at his side; it has grown beyond its once rational limits, swollen in a kind of world-destroying acromegaly, gone knobby and awkward and bizarre, gone self-destructive, gone more than a little mad. None of this can be what Truman intended; but what has happened is the result of the groundwork he laid. Present at the creation indeed: present now in the days before the flood, or perhaps the apocalyptic fire, blunt phallic ABMs raining genetic death on a race that murders to create.

What does a President do when he leaves office? How can he bear the loss of power and authority? John Kennedy was lucky; he died and passed over immediately into myth. Eisenhower was a myth before he ever took office: no sweat. Hoover's Quakerism saved him, and his training as an engineer; he lived on to become the nation's most efficient vacuum cleaner, Hoovering up the starving refugees of World War II, Hoovering up the administrative mess of the war-swollen federal government, passing everything through his ample bag and leaving the rug of state decently clean. Lyndon Johnson will bear the loss the worst of them all; presently he broods in the cavern of his guarded top-floor offices, spewing forth memoirs like a stricken whale gushing blood.

Truman solved the problem as only he could. He became a high-school teacher. First he wrote his memoirs, then he buried himself in the details of building and establishing a Presidential library, then he taught school. His Library, on

I-70 north of Independence, is laid out like a study unit for a civics course, with curios thrown in to hold the kids' attention. A major exhibit is devoted to the six jobs of the President as Truman defines them: Chief Executive, ceremonial chief of state, legislative planner, head of his political party, commander in chief of the Armed Forces, and director of foreign policy. Around this central exhibit are grouped others remarkable only for their naïveté.

In one wing, plunked down on the bare limestone floor, sits Harry's pre-war Chrysler, the car in which he conducted his Senatorial reelection campaign in 1940, drove as Senator and then as Vice President, and turned over to his sister when he became President. She drove it from 1945 to 1951, frugal as he. The Chrysler Corporation later had it restored; pale green, with those impossibly large balloon tires cars used to wear, it still shows the hammered-out remains of fender dents earned careening down Missouri back roads and in the maze of Washington, D.C., traffic.

Thomas Hart Benton's mural, "Independence and the Opening of the West," three years in the making and painted with bravura right onto the wall by crafty old Tom, glows across from the Library's main entrance, a swollen montage of settlers and Indians rising to a peak over a large double doorway, an orgy of aniline in the plain limestone-and-marble hall.

Truman's White House office is preserved more or less intact in one wing, and by pressing a button you may hear the President himself explain to you the details of the room, the hidden doors, the furnishings. In such a setting one wishes Disney's Imagineers would construct an audio-animatronic Truman to deliver the lecture in person, banging his plastic fist on the desk to drive each point home. The single black telephone on the Presidential desk appears deficient and antique after the supercommunication systems of Kennedy and

85

Johnson. But all is not authentic in the Truman Library Oval Room. Surely Truman did not fill the White House's shelves with the hundred-volume history of Brazil in Portuguese that lines the wall nearest the visitors' bay?

Visitors, says the museum's curator, like best the 12' by 17' Persian rug that hangs opposite the stairwell in the museum, all 29 million knots of it, a gift to Truman from the Shah of Iran. They also like the ornamental swords encased near the main entrance, heavy with jewels. The White House floor beam which sagged under the weight of Margaret Truman's piano, cracked and dusty and ensconced in a glass case as if it were the Declaration of Independence, amuses visitors, as it must amuse Harry.

He himself no longer visits the Library. He used to be there every day at 7:45 sharp after a brisk one-mile walk from the Wallace house, due north to the Library through an old and quiet Independence neighborhood. His constituency in those days, the late fifties and early sixties, was children, bussed out by the hundreds from area schools to see a live President turned civics instructor. One May the museum curator kept count of the groups Harry spoke to: one hundred in one month. He would take on four or five bunches a day, cracking out sharp answers to their questions about tough decisions, about how to be good citizens. "Korea, Korea," he would tell them, still brooding on the deaths of that undeclared war, and "Read, read," he would tell them, knowing how far reading had gotten him over the years, what a good citizen it had made of him. He would autograph someone's cast and drag along visiting dignitaries to answer the kids' questions and to show the visitors that the Chief still had a constituency of sorts, albeit sans body hair. He would steadfastly refuse to discuss foreign policy, disclaiming knowledge of the facts but really remembering how damned difficult such partisan discussions had made his own Presidential years. Ah, they were star performances, his appearances before those uncritical awed audiences, and they did him a world of good.

Grownups came too, tourists from all over the country. It was a quick stop right there on the Interstate like a Howard Johnson's halfway between New York and California and maybe we'll catch a glimpse of old Harry himself. Admissions fell off at the Library when Harry began staying home; people would drive by the Wallace house instead, hoping to see the old man on his side porch or out walking.

The real riches of the Library no one sees except the six hundred scholars and journalists who have signed in over the years at the back door. In the stacks, boxes upon boxes of Presidential papers stand in neat rows like massed troops, a total of six million sheets of paper. The juiciest are unavailable for reading, and will remain so until the people who wrote them and the people about whom they are written are dead and gone and no feelings left to be hurt. Each box is fumigated as it arrives, as if to fix it in a permanent present. Digging through a few of the boxes, you sense the enormity of the American Presidency better than you can by talking to a President or pressing buttons in the Oval Room: letters of pride and heartbreak from ordinary citizens, numberless memos, drafts of speeches, handwritten notes, the minutely detailed history of an era. "The great period for Truman research lies ahead of us," says the Truman Library's director of research and records. "Ten years ahead. The Roosevelt period is just now coming available." Some of the most important papers have not even arrived in Independence yet: Acheson's, for example. And some won't: Jimmy Byrnes', who never liked Harry anyway because he thought Harry stole the Presidency from him.

But writing memoirs, building a library, and giving civics instruction were never enough, could never be enough for a man who ran the world for seven years. "I hope you will remember what I have been," he told an audience at the New

York World's Fair in 1964, "and not what I am today." He walked into the Jackson County Courthouse in Kansas City one day—he built that courthouse when he was Presiding Judge of the Court, an administrative position. The three Judges who run the county's business greeted him warmly enough, and he told them, "I just happened to be downtown and heard you were meeting and came over to see if an old man out of a job could get work."

He felt the deprivation keenly. He had no hobbies; he had no sports; when reporters tried to characterize him after his nomination from obscurity as Vice President in 1944, he told them simply, "I'm a workhorse." Out to pasture, the workhorse cast about for something to do. One of the curious results of Truman's retirement was *Mr. Citizen*, a book as bare of substance as his two-volume *Memoirs* was crammed. In *Mr. Citizen* he discusses his friends, his operations, his grandchildren, his travels, and then makes a panicky plea for something to do:

> Congress should pass enabling legislation designating former Presidents of the United States *as Free Members of Congress.*
>
> These Free Members would have the right to sit on the floor of the Senate and of the House on all occasions.
>
> They would have the right to take part in debate, subject, of course, to the parliamentary procedures in each house.
>
> The Free Members *would not have the right to vote.*
>
> They *would* have the right to sit in on any meetings of any committee, subcommittee, or joint committee of both houses and take part in discussions. Here, too, they would not have the right to vote.
>
> Free Members would be assigned suitable office space in the Congressional buildings.

88

But without the right to vote, without a constituency behind them except for such national goodwill as remains after a President leaves office, what possible authority would Truman's Free Members possess? Or think of it this way: can you imagine Lyndon Johnson a Free Member?

(Notice that in the midst of this momentous proposal the ever-practical Truman provides for office space. He alone among twentieth-century Presidents actually saved money out of his Presidential salary—saved as much as a quarter of a million dollars, by one estimate.)

The pastured workhorse wrote a newspaper column for a while in 1964, but inexplicably stopped. When they laid the foundations for the Churchill Memorial Chapel in Fulton, Missouri, in 1964, Harry was on hand to turn a golden shovelful of dirt. Westminster College announced at that time an $80,000 gift to establish the Harry S. Truman Chair of American History, and said that Truman himself would deliver the first eight lectures. He never did. That same year, augur of decline, Vergne Dixon of Dixon's Chili Parlor in Kansas City, where President Truman was wont to dine, died of a heart attack.

By 1966 Truman was reported at home suffering dizzy spells, and one reporter claimed the former President had Parkinson's disease. Truman's family physician, Dr. Wallace Graham, denied the claim, although Graham was quoted in a letter to the director of the National Parkinson Foundation as referring to a "Parkinson-like syndrome." What Truman did have was a tendency to vertigo whenever he stood on his feet very long; that more than anything else was responsible for his discontinuing his daily visits to the Library and his regular daily walks.

The traditionally Republican Citizens Party officials of Kansas City, Missouri, had never liked Truman. In 1967, when the city council was ready to name the new international airport under construction north of Kansas City, the councilmen hurriedly approved the name "Kansas City International" to avoid discussion of the name "Harry S. Truman International," discussion which might offend the former President. "What has Harry ever done for Kansas City?" was the tone of the meeting, a *Kansas City Star* reporter thought. Meanwhile the airlines, believing the airport would be named Midcontinent International, printed up millions of baggage tickets boldly marked MCI.

By 1969 Truman had visited the hospital again to recover from a bout of flu. Influenza was epidemic across the United States that winter. He went to Key West to recover, a successful trip. The same year, a Kansas City businessman named Alex Barket spent $80,850 on a railroad car claimed by its San Francisco owner to be the *Ferdinand Magellan*, the car on which Harry conducted his Give-Em-Hell whistle-stop campaign of 1948. Barket proposed to make the car available for static display, and spent a good deal of money refurbishing it, but the car's lineage soon came into question: it may have been a car in which Truman once rode, but it was probably not the car used in the campaign. Chagrined, Barket claimed he still believed his car was the *Ferdinand Magellan*, and anyway he could get his money back if it was not an authentic relic.

Harry S. Truman was eighty-five in 1969. He had pledged at eighty that he would live to be ninety. Once or twice each year, rumors fly around Kansas City that he is dead or dying at Research Hospital, his favorite, now a brand-new building and air-conditioned throughout. The rumors suggest that the people of the area are through with the living man and anxious to get on with the business of honoring his death—keeping up with Abilene, as it were.

And today Independence seems a town dispossessed, as if, Truman declining, it were being dismantled and carried away. It labored mightily to bring forth a great city, but brought forth something infinitely more valuable: a great man. It hardly recognizes him as such, knowing as it does the ground from which he came, but he is its finest issue. Behind Memorial Hall sits a cupola, white wooden dome over a brick foundation. For years it housed a replica of the Liberty Bell given to Independence by the town of Annecy le Vieux, France. Walking back from the Wallace house, I discover that the cupola is empty, the bell gone, the bronze plaque rudely torn out of its brick moorings. I wonder where the bell has gone,* as I wonder where the Watson Memorial Methodist Church has gone that no mark of its presence is left. On the square the courthouse is dilapidated, the windows dirty and spattered with paint, the sidewalk broken and faulted and bristling with aging parking meters. The equestrian statue of Andrew Jackson, the county's namesake, rides like a late commuter toward the bus stop on the southeastern corner of the square, and across the street discount stores and empty store fronts bleat urban decay. Somewhere along the way, breeding pioneers and gunmen and one mighty President, Independence lost its soul.

What is it, then, to be very old and to have been President of the United States in the sixth decade of the second century of their federation? It is to live in a body musted like old books, a shrunken body that no longer fills the clothes you wear, the shirt collars hanging from the neck, the pants baggy at the seat, the coat drooping over the ends of your contracted shoulders. Your body no longer responds; sluggish, cranky, it demands your attention, requires you to think about where next to place your foot for safety because the bones are brittle now and you can break your hip just stepping off a curb. It is to find your tongue sucking your front

* To the lawn of the Truman Library, as it turns out, where Liberty is rung in again by the Boy Scouts each Fourth of July.

teeth like some lizard you have caught that fights to get away, lunging and lunging as you struggle to hold it still without pinching it into pain. It is to see a different face in the mirror every morning, a face shrunken at the cheeks, eyes looking out of deep cones created by the wasting away of subcutaneous fat, eyes with pupils constricted by your ever-present anger at being old, eyes that you have looked at too long and that now seem to look back at you with a despair you by now take for granted.

And to be old is to know that within this moldering shell which you once propelled proudly down miles of sidewalks at exactly 120 paces per minute, your brain is still alive and functioning, slower now, some of its nooks and crannies harder to reach, some of its cupboards bare that once opened onto home-canned riches of memory and logic and imagination, but still capable of so much more thought than your body can act upon that each sluggish response must make you mad. And so signals of anger flash back through the still-clear circuits, and you must recycle or unravel or suppress the anger or risk overloading the entire system and breaking down in simple rage—and you are someone who was never known for keeping your temper if you didn't want to.

Stored in that brain, stuck in that brain with no earthly value now (because the last thing anyone wants in America is an old man, especially an old man who once controlled vast power and thus can no longer be deferential to any man except perhaps another President, and probably not even one of those, since they don't make them the way they used to any more), stored in that brain is this enormous bank of data about the history of the world, American and British and French and German history and probably Tibetan and Angolese history as well. And nothing to do with it, no place to use it, no decisions to make out of this walking library loaded to the gunwales with good men and bad, good decisions and bad, sly Elizabethan ploys and hidden Napoleonic mistresses and stupid battle maneuvers and ships' cargo lists and gunpowder plots on all seven continents and the toilet habits of every American President and the exact number of bottles of wine that caused the downfall of the Roman Empire and all the words you had in secret and in public with the most powerful and the most brilliant men of your time.

And behind that synaptic bank of data another bank reserved for your long quiet relationship with the woman you honored and respected and possibly even loved for half a century, and with a little girl grown to be an intelligent and pleasant matron.

And behind that bank another bank, loamier, misted, with farm animals and distant cousins and the names of country trees and the way it felt to ride a horse on an October morning in Grandview, Missouri, before anyone ever heard of horseless carriages, much less atomic bombs.

"I hope you will remember what I have been and not what I am today." All the depth of it is there, the chill and pinch of age, the sorrow and sadness and bitterness and anger. Once you cheered a staff of good and sturdy men who worshiped your power and respected your good sense; now your one secretary, aging too and prim, sits in the office you can no longer visit and keeps the light on through the day. Once Presidents and Prime Ministers, Emperors and Kings, Ambassadors ordinary and extraordinary, Senators and Representatives, heads of great departments of government, Generals and Admirals, captains of industry, poets and journalists, winners of Nobel Prizes and earnest brilliant scientists, ordinary citizens, young people, deferred to you, hung on your every word, nodded and blushed and smiled; now an occasional President stops by your door, often enough a man you detest on principle and for a fact, and you come to the door because you still feel the office deserves that obeisance despite riots and murderous undeclared wars (you had one yourself, but you won it and won it as clean as such wars can be won and probably think you could win in Viet Nam too, but only God could do that). And other than Presidents giving you the time of day because they want someone to give them the time of day when they also are old, you see only intimate visitors, and few enough of those.

You never gave a damn for the fussy protocols of office anyway, not for yourself as Independence boy, though you certainly gave a damn about them for yourself as Chief Executive Officer. You learned that schizoid distinction as an officer in the war if not earlier as the elected head of the Independence Treehouse Association. But if you didn't care for protocol, you loved to see the people, like every politician and every decent statesman, loved to feel the massed weight of their bodies crowding around like ballots raised out of the valley of dry bones into flesh. You could govern so vast a country, so various a country, so fickle and coy and sometimes vicious a country, because you were a one-man cross-section, small-town boy and country boy, soldier and dapper businessman, practical county judge and shrewd politician, self-taught historian and steel-rimmed facts-and-figures Senator and snappy tough-minded President all rolled into one, with a whiff of the barnyard and a squirt of the church usher thrown in for good measure. You could dine with the Achesons and not eat your salad with your dinner fork and you could hunker down with a tough old farmer and bite off a hefty plug of Red Man and not choke. You were a countryman first and last and always, but you knew your way around.

And now he sits in his study, a small study, surrounded by books, reading books, reading a book a day (not some light-hearted novel or detective story, either, but a wordy historical study, the latest poop on the battle of Agincourt, the definitive printing of Abraham Lincoln's little-known early epic

94

poems)—books and more books, so many books that Bess
can't keep up with him despite the flood of new titles
shipped out to Independence by unctuous New York pub-
lishers hoping for a quote, and must send out panic calls to
friends like a little Dutch girl with her finger in the dike,
More books, more books, Harry wants more books.

The memoirs are finished, the peculiar inhibited confes-
sion of ordinary citizenship is dry on the shelves of public
libraries, not much checked out any more; the study of Presidents never completed, the newspaper column abandoned,
the lectures never given, the other books he wanted to write
that he never told anyone about, books about the nature of
the Presidency and the nature of history and the nature of
the universe never written; still he sits in that little study behind those thick glasses reading, reading, just as he did as a
boy, reading, storing up even more facts, weighing each decision, playing President down all the corridors of history, no
longer confined to that oval office with the plow on the desk
and the secret secretarial doors and THE BUCK STOPS HERE and
the slicker mob of newsmen cooling their hot feet in the cor-
ridor waiting to catch him swearing again.

And all that reading useless now except to pass back and
forth before his eyes for casual entertainment like a marathon
Hollywood production, the events of history fading in and
out of each other so that he can visit Waterloo with Caesar
on the sidelines and confer with Napoleon about what he
ought to do; visit Atlanta with MacArthur—no, not that son-
of-a-bitch MacArthur—with Hannibal to advise Robert E.
Lee about the advantages of elephants; walk down Pennsyl-
vania Avenue with Lincoln at his side, Lincoln taking half as
many steps to cover the same ground, Truman looking up at
him but not deferring to him at all, Washington loping along
behind, lost in ponderous Germanic thought, Truman snub-
bing the weakling Zachary Taylor as he passes, waving at

95

Jackson and giving him a wink that says *We understand these city boys*, Truman's petite thin-soled rich-man's shoes clicking away the pavement under him; or he can mount his pony and go out and look for stretches of pasture beyond the windbreak where he can ride hell-for-leather just like Teddy's Rough Riders and no doting mother on hand to worry about his losing his glasses or breaking a leg.

And all the other flashing pictures, all of William James's wonderful stream of our consciousness that becomes paradoxically such a comfort and such a bitter burden now, the aching emptiness of the White House when Truman was alone at night and his wife and daughter were away; the warm Florida sun; the good bawdy jokes, all the thousands of them, that he told over the years to win the confidence of those seemingly manly, seemingly strong, big-jawed and big-chested men who were in fact little boys in need of Truman's strength, he more a man than any of them despite his small size and scratchy baritone, he tough as nails and stringy as a coyote on a cold day in March.

If he is very lucky, he doesn't know any more that he is merely sitting in his study in Independence. If he is very lucky, he believes he is sitting in the Athenian Senate holding a conference with Disraeli and Tom Jefferson and Jim Bridger and Attila the Hun. But probably he is aware; friends report he's as sharp as ever, though who believes friends? But probably he knows, knows his age now who never knew it before, who became Senator in 1935 at the age of fifty-one and President in 1945 at the age of sixty-one. Probably he knows that he is dying.

But if he knows, as any man must finally know it, as every man feels his body sinking downward into death in a gradual descent that brings real fear because he never knows the day and hour it will happen (and even if he doesn't fear pain he still must fear that final cessation, though in those final moments if he has lived well he will cease to fear the rest); if he knows, if Harry S. Truman knows that he is dying, then why is he still preparing for the next great test of his ability to make big decisions and make them right by reading, reading, reading? But then again, why not? He prepared that way all his life, while the slick boys were out cutting a figure. He probably believes in an afterlife, and expects at very least to be one of Heaven's Free Members. And tough he always was, smart he always was, ready for the next challenge he always was, crude he sometimes was, but slick? Never. Harry Truman, Jesse James, Mark Twain: as Dr. Billy G. Hurt might say, Father, Son, and Holy Ghost. Amen.

5 Behold, How Good and How Pleasant It Is for Brethren to Dwell Together in Unity*

THE UNITY SCHOOL OF PRACTICAL CHRISTIANITY, IN LEE'S SUM-
mit, Missouri, is a profoundly American institution. It was
founded on prayer, and still lives by it. The School's department of Silent Unity shipped out more than 700,000 prayers
to the world last year, all of them in answer to personal requests. More than 6,000 letters, telegrams, and telephone calls
reach the Silent Unity building each day. A second-story window in the building glows perpetually; inside is a telephone
room where workers answer calls around the clock. Long before suicide centers, poison-control centers, and Dial-a-Priest,

* *Psalm* 133:1.

Unity waited patiently for your call, and waits at this moment.

"There were three connecting rooms," writes Dr. Marcus Bach in *The Unity Way of Life*, a Prentice-Hall book, "but the one I recalled this night was the one with the perpetually burning light, the votive light of prayer. There was a large round table in the center of that room, divided into arcs and equipped with telephones, and there were workers answering the calls in quiet tones, and I thought I heard them give thanks to those who called that every need is already fulfilled." That is Unity's sort of prayer, positive and affirmative and a little wacky, and it has its reward.

Prayer requests account for half of Unity's income; testimonials returned to Unity by those who believe themselves helped usually contain a gift of money—a "love offering," in Unity's term. The other half of Unity's income comes from subscriptions to its several periodicals, which are more or less self-supporting. *Daily Word*, a monthly calendar of scriptural meditations, is the best known.

"Silent Unity," says an officer of the School, "generates a great number of free-will offerings. Support for what I call our 'outreach' programs comes this way. These buildings were built that way. The property was acquired that way." But Unity does not disclose financial figures. "It's not that they're secret," the officer says. "We just can't see what good it would do." The Internal Revenue Service, he points out, reapproved their tax-exempt status some years back. The size of Unity's operations and the number of its employees suggest income of several millions a year.

"The prayer work is the thing that made Unity," according to James Dillet Freeman of Unity. Freeman is a handsome man of middle height and middle age. Iced with silver-gray hair, dressed in suede and corduroy, he looks the American poet whom he believes himself to be. Like many public lecturers, he speaks English when discussing the spirit, American when discussing the flesh. He believes in the Unity movement, and has given it his life. He is its historian, its permanent poet-in-residence, and a teacher at its School.

"Prayer attracted the people," he explains. "Healing is still a big item. The thing about this place—and this is true—is that it's always attracted people who very much believed in what they were doing—the people in charge are people who themselves are utterly convinced that they're serving—that their prayers are effective. Unity maintains a constant, round-the-clock prayer watch. They used to pass a picture of Jesus Christ from desk to desk. If the picture came on your desk, then you went into the prayer room and prayed until somebody else came in. There's no cynicism here.

"We have two things to give people," Freeman continues. "One is a feeling of faith—we are praying with you. You're not alone. Two, you're *loved*—here's somebody thinking of you, caring for you, interested in you and your welfare. Most human beings need these—pretty strongly. If we did nothing else than this, we'd do enough. These are the great things we've got to give people. Probably 650,000 people contact us every year. Most of it is word of mouth. Somebody is in trouble and someone tells them about us."

Unity maintains its perpetual prayer watch in a chapel down the hall from the telephone room. Workers drop prayer requests into baskets at the front of the chapel, where they absorb prayers for a month or so before being removed. "I think they stay there about sixty days now," Freeman says. That is a powerful dose of a sovereign remedy. Years ago, Unity printed a healing prayer on a red insert page in its monthly magazine; overzealous believers physically applied what they called the "red leaf" to their afflictions. Unity chided them for the practice, but gently, for who knows the ways of God? Prayer, tapping the free energies of the universe, may well work as a metaphysical unguent, a subtle and cosmic Ben-Gay.

Unity reaches out with many limbs. The School trains workers for Unity's churches (called "centers" to avoid any whiff of denomination) and publishes the organization's many books, periodicals, and leaflets in its own printing plant. Silent Unity handles prayer and healing requests. Silent 70, named from Luke 10:1 (*After these things the Lord appointed other seventy also, and sent them two and two before his face into every city and place, whither he himself would come*), supplies free Unity magazines, tracts, and books to the prisons of America. The Braille department makes Unity materials available to the blind. The Department of World Unity spreads the Good Word across the world, and lately, according to Unity spokesmen, is making great inroads in England, where church attendance is down to a bare three percent of the population.

The past shadows the present, at Unity as throughout the Midwest. The traditional European forms of Christian worship—the cathedral and the priest, the solid stone church and the solid stone pastor—never were available in quantity on the frontier, and it could not have sat still for them if they were. Midwestern settlers wanted Higher Guidance; not finding it in traditional religion, which only reluctantly moved west, they devised their own. They injected religion into business and invented the Chamber of Commerce, into politics and invented Honest Government, into personal behavior and invented the Dale Carnegie Course. They didn't completely give up their Christianity, but they expected it, as William James did, to perform. The turn of the century was high tide for this new-time religion. It stirred more sentiment than passion. James Sheldon's *In His Steps*, written out of Topeka, Kansas, began its climb to all-time best-sellerdom in 1906, proposing that each of us literally follow Jesus' example, and many tried, including the founders of Unity, to the best of their understanding. When *In His Steps* came to town by lecture and lantern slide, grown women wept. New Thought steamed out of Boston and New York and Chicago on the 20th Century Limited; Mary Baker Eddy's pinched, Bostonian Christian Science began building its mock-Episcopal fortresses; healers roamed the countryside with magic incantations and bottomless pocketbooks, and the Midwest turned on.

A businessman and his wife founded Unity. Charles Fillmore was a real-estate salesman who dabbled in gold mining, popular science, and comparative religion at a time when all three were rich in undiscovered lodes. Fillmore might never have left real estate if his ingenious and attractive wife, Myrtle, hadn't got interested in faith healing. In her letters, published after Unity was well under way, she would gently insist that she had started the movement. She had, but her husband made it work.

Charles Fillmore was born in a log cabin on an Indian reservation in Minnesota in 1854. A Sioux medicine man carried him off for the day when he was only two years old. "Where they had taken him and what they had done with him, Charles could not remember," James Freeman writes in his history of Unity, "but he always had a feeling that they had used him in some mystical ceremony." When Charles was seven, his trader father moved to another cabin ten miles away, and after that the boy and his younger brother Norton divided their time between the cabins of their parents. They harvested wild rice, Indian-style; they wandered among the lodges, witnessing who knows what oddities of living; they got little schooling.

Norton ran away to the West at a tender age and never returned. Charles dislocated his hip one day in a skating accident. The leg failed to set properly, and developed a bone infection. "I was bled, leeched, cupped, lanced, seasoned, blistered, and roweled," Fillmore later told Freeman. "Six running sores were artificially produced on my leg to draw out the diseased condition that was presumed to be within. Physicians of different schools were employed, and the last one always wondered how I ever pulled through alive under the treatment of the 'quack' that preceded him; and as I look back at it now it's a miracle to me how I ever got away from them all with the little bundle of bones and sinews that I found in my possession after they had finished their experiments."

The leg withered and grew no more. All his life, "Papa Charley," as Unity workers called Charles Fillmore, would pray the leg longer, though there is little evidence that it responded.

When he was old enough to leave home, Fillmore went to work as a printer's devil in St. Cloud, Minnesota. He worked in a grocery store and a bank. He befriended the son of an Army officer, and the boy's college-educated mother—a rarity in those days—plied her son's bright friend with books—Shakespeare, Tennyson, Emerson, Lowell, Whittier. Much later, Charles would name one of his sons Waldo Rickert, another Lowell, in honor of his beloved transcendentalists, and there is much of New England mysticism in Unity, oddly blended, as it oddly blends, with Christianity.

In St. Cloud, Fillmore read about the West and found it challenging. He traveled to Denison, Texas, a town reputed to be as rough as they came in those days, but it was at a literary-society meeting in Denison that Charles met the red-headed schoolteacher, Myrtle Page, who would later become his wife. She had attended Oberlin College. She believed she had inherited tuberculosis. She had unusual religious ideas. When she returned to Clinton, Missouri, to teach school, Charles courted her with letters and books.

He lost his job in Denison and went north to Colorado, where he became a mule-team driver, studied assaying, and started to deal in real estate. He plucked Myrtle out of Missouri after marrying her there in 1881. In Pueblo, Colorado, Fillmore & Company, Realtors, temporarily prospered. "Charles's partner at that time was Charles Small, brother-in-law of Nona Brooks, who later founded Divine Science," remarks Freeman. The forces were gathering that early.

In 1884, the Fillmore family, now increased by two sons, moved to Kansas City, Missouri, then in the midst of a building boom. Charles Fillmore laid out a real-estate subdivision named Gladstone Heights, which still stands. It includes Myrtle Avenue, named for his wife, and Norton Avenue, named for his wandering brother. Charles packed the family one summer and went prospecting for silver in Colorado. He found a vein, but it quickly petered out. Back in Kansas City, the real-estate boom collapsed; simultaneously, Myrtle's tuberculosis flared up. "Her son Lowell," says Freeman, "recalls that the medicine cabinet was always full to overflowing with pills and nostrums with which she was continually dosing herself and all the other members of the family."

Ever restless, the Fillmores attended lectures. One they turned out for was delivered by a student of a woman who had worked with Mary Baker Eddy. The lecturer's main assertion buoyed Myrtle Fillmore's hope. She was in the right place at the right time. "I am a child of God," the lecturer announced, "and therefore I do not inherit sickness." Myrtle, believer in pills and nostrums, discovered a new faith: that statement founded Unity.

"It flashed upon me," she wrote later, "that I might talk to the life in every part of my body and have it do just what I wanted. I began to teach my body and got marvelous results." "In just two years," writes Freeman, "Myrtle Fillmore was no longer an invalid. Through her prayers she was made absolutely whole."

Take that statement for what you will, Myrtle lived a long and healthy life.

People heard of Myrtle's miraculous healing and came to her for counsel. Charles was less easily convinced. "Although I was a chronic invalid and seldom free from pain," he wrote later, "the doctrine did not at first appeal to me." Two years later, finding the doctrine more appealing, Fillmore published the first issue of a little magazine called *Modern Thought*, "Devoted to the Spiritualization of Humanity from an Independent Standpoint." In the interim, his income had declined and a third child had been born.

Modern Thought received a small number of love offerings and became *Christian Science Thought*, a more specific name. Papa Charley wrangled long with Mary Baker Eddy about his use of that then-generic term. Mrs. Eddy wanted to keep "Christian Science" for her exclusive use. Fillmore thought otherwise: "People of limited spiritual unfoldment," he wrote in his magazine, "are sticklers for names and creeds, and are thus worshippers of idols. . . . They quarrel over names, names, names, vapid, unmeaning names, that never were anything of themselves and do not even represent that which they allege to represent." But he gave in to Mrs. Eddy at last and rechristened his magazine *Thought*.

Quarrel over names who may, the Fillmore movement still lacked one—lacked what we might today call brand identity. Charles generated the missing name out of a prayer meeting one night, when he and Myrtle and a circle of students had "gone into the silence," as they called meditation. Freeman recaptures the excitement:

"That's it!" he cried out. "UNITY!" he told the others. "UNITY! that's the name for our work, the name we've been looking for."

Later he told friends the name came right out of the ether, just as the voice of Jesus was heard by Paul in the